REVISE EDEXCEL GCSE
German
REVISION GUIDE

D0532998

Series Consultant: Harry Smith   Author: Harriette Lanzer

THE REVISE EDEXCEL SERIES
Available in print or online

Online editions for all titles in the Revise Edexcel series are available Summer 2013.

Presented on our ActiveLearn platform, you can view the full book and customise it by adding notes, comments and weblinks.

Print editions

German Revision Guide   9781446903421

German Revision Workbook   9781446903483

Online editions

German Revision Guide   9781446903452

German Revision Workbook   9781446903322

This Revision Guide is designed to complement your classroom and home learning, and to help prepare you for the exam. It does not include all the content and skills needed for the complete course. It is designed to work in combination with Edexcel's main GCSE German 2009 Series.

Audio files
Audio files for the listening exercises in this book can be found at: www.pearsonschools.co.uk/mflrevisionaudio

To find out more visit:
www.pearsonschools.co.uk/edexcelgcseMFLrevision

ALWAYS LEARNING   **PEARSON**

Contents

Audio files

Audio files for the listening exercises in this book can be found at: www.pearsonschools.co.uk/mflrevisionaudio

A small bit of small print

Edexcel publishes Sample Assessment Material and the Specification on its website. This is the official content and this book should be used in conjunction with it. The questions in *Now try this* have been written to help you practise every topic in the book. Remember: the real exam questions may not look like this.

Target grades

Target grades are quoted in this book for some of the questions. Students targeting this grade should be aiming to get most of the marks available. Students targeting a higher grade should be aiming to get all of the marks available.

Birthdays

Make sure you can recognise months and dates. Learn these topics well to avoid mistaking a month or number.

Geburtstage

Januar   Februar   März   April

Mai   Juni   Juli   August

September   Oktober   November   Dezember

Ich habe am vierten Mai Geburtstag.
My birthday is on 4th May.

Ich bin / wurde am dritten August 2001 geboren.
I was born on 3rd August 2001.

Dates

> Grammar page 110

14 → am → Juli

am + date + month –
am vierzehnten Juli

im

↓

im + month – im Juli

When you say a year, just use numbers. There is no word for 'in':
in 2010 – zweitausendzehn
in 1999 – neunzehnhundertneunundneunzig
Note also: im Jahr 2012.

Audio files

Audio files can be found at:
www.pearsonschools.co.uk/mflrevisionaudio

Worked example

LISTENING 1   **target E**

When is Christian's birthday? Put a cross by the correct date.
(a) 27th May ☐   **(b)** 16th June ☐   **(c)** 26th June ☒

– Wann hast du Geburtstag, Christian?
– Ich habe am sechsundzwanzigsten Juni Geburtstag. Das ist am Sonntag!

Learning dates

Dates and numbers are really important so make sure you are confident with them.

You're looking for **two** pieces of information – the date and the month.

Now try this

LISTENING 2   **target E**

Listen to three more people and put a cross by the correct date:

1 (a) 20th October ☐   **(b)** 30th October ☐   **(c)** 30th November ☐
2 (a) 17th May ☐   **(b)** 7th May ☐   **(c)** 27th May ☐
3 (a) 29th May ☐   **(b)** 19th March ☐   **(c)** 29th March ☐

Don't get confused between **Mai** (May) and **März** (March). Listen twice: once for the **date**, once for the **month**. Then you could try to note the **year** for extra practice.

Had a look ☐ Nearly there ☐ Nailed it! ☐

Physical description

In the speaking assessment you will need to describe yourself accurately if asked ... but in the writing assessment you can describe your dream self!

Wie sehe ich aus?

Ich habe ... Haare

blonde   graue

braune   schwarze

dunkle / helle	dark / light
glatte / lockige	straight / curly
kurze / lange	short / long
Ich habe (blaue) Augen.	I have (blue) eyes.
Ich trage eine Brille.	I wear glasses.
Sie trägt große Ohrringe.	She wears big earrings.
Er hat einen Bart / Schnurrbart.	He's got a beard / moustache.
Sie hat ein rundes Gesicht.	She's got a round face.
Ich habe eine lange Nase.	I've got a long nose.

Comparing things
Grammar page 92

- For regular comparatives add -er to the adjective:

attraktiv ➡	attraktiver
dick(er)	fat(ter)
hässlich(er)	ugly (uglier)
hübsch(er)	pretty (prettier)
schlank(er)	slim(mer)
schön(er)	(more) beautiful

- The following are irregular:

alt ➡	älter	(old / older)
groß ➡	größer	(big / bigger)
gut ➡	besser	(good / better)
hoch ➡	höher	(high / higher)
jung ➡	jünger	(young / younger)

- Use als to compare:

Ich bin älter als du. I am older than you.

Worked example
READING · target E

Read the text.

> Der Verdächtige ist ein Jugendlicher im Alter von siebzehn Jahren mit langen, dunkelbraunen Haaren und einem Ziegenbart. Er trägt einen kleinen Ohrring im linken Ohr und hat eine Narbe auf der Nase.

Put a cross in the correct box.

The suspect is ...

(a) a 17-year-old male. ☒

(b) a 7-year-old male. ☐

(c) a 17-year-old female. ☐

- Circle or underline key words to help you focus – here, they are **Der Verdächtige** (suspect) and **siebzehn Jahren** (17 years).
- Even if you don't know the word **Verdächtige**, the fact that it is a **der** word tells you this is a male person.

Don't be confused by words like **Ziegenbart** (goatee) – the **bart** part of the word should be enough to tell you this person has a beard of some description.

Now try this
READING · target E

Complete these sentences about the above text by putting a cross in the correct box.

1 The suspect has ...

(a) long light brown hair. ☐

(b) long black hair. ☐

(c) long dark brown hair. ☐

2 He has ...

(a) an earring and glasses. ☐

(b) a goatee and an earring. ☐

(c) a goatee and glasses. ☐

3 On his nose there is ...

(a) a scar. ☐

(b) a piercing. ☐

(c) a spot. ☐

Character description

To talk about character, you need to know the verb sein and lots of adjectives.

Charakterbeschreibung

Ich bin ...	I am ...
altmodisch	old-fashioned
blöd	silly
böse	angry / cross
egoistisch	selfish
ehrlich	honest
ernst	serious
frech	cheeky
gemein	mean / nasty
großartig	awesome
hilfsbereit	helpful
komisch	funny
lebhaft	lively
lieb	likeable / nice
nervig	annoying
nett	nice
sauer	cross
schüchtern	shy
witzig	funny / witty
Ich bin humorlos.	I have no sense of humour.

The verb sein (to be)

ich	bin	I am
du	bist	you are
er / sie / es	ist	he / she / it is
wir	sind	we are
ihr	seid	you are
Sie / sie	sind	you / they are

Imperfect tense

ich war (I was) sie waren (they were)

Eva ist intelligent, aber faul.

You may well need to distinguish between past and present characteristics:

Obwohl er heute frech ist, war er als Kind sehr schüchtern. Although he **is** cheeky today, he **was** very shy as a child.

Worked example

 LISTENING 3   target D

Daniel is describing his best friend Thomas. Put a cross by the word which applies to him.

funny ☒   noisy ☐   lazy ☐

– Thomas ist sehr lustig, aber er geht nicht gern mit einer Gruppe Freunden aus. Das findet er zu laut.

Aiming higher

Give your work an edge by including one or two of these Higher level adjectives in your writing / speaking.

angeberisch	pretentious
ausgeglichen	well-balanced
deprimiert	depressed
eingebildet	conceited
großzügig	generous
selbstbewusst	self-confident
verrückt	mad / crazy
zuverlässig	reliable

Now try this

 LISTENING 4   target D

Listen to the rest of the description and put a cross by the **four** correct letters which describe Thomas.

A keen on sport	☐	D lazy	☐	G understanding	☐
B messy	☐	E generous		H impatient	☐
C sometimes bad tempered	☐	F noisy	☐		

ID

Check you can give your personal information if asked. You will find nationalities on page 5.

Der Personalausweis

Alter (n)	age
Geschlecht (n)	gender / sex
Junge (m) / Mädchen (n)	boy / girl
Vorname (m)	first name
Familienname (m)	surname
Spitzname (m)	nickname
Geburtsdatum (n)	date of birth
Geburtsort (m)	place of birth
Postleitzahl (f)	postcode
Telefonnummer (f)	phone number
Staatsangehörigkeit (f)	nationality
Adresse / Anschrift (f)	address
Wohnort (m)	place of residence
Doppelhaus (n)	semi-detached house
Einfamilienhaus (n)	detached house
Reihenhaus (n)	terraced house
Wohnung (f)	flat

The alphabet

Try to speak German words clearly and with a good accent. Use the listening passages from this book to help practise pronunciation.

A ah	Ä ah umlaut	B beh	ß ess-testt	C tseh	D deh
E eh	F eff	G geh	H ha	I ee	J yat
K kah	L ell	M emm	N enn	O oh	Ö oh umlaut
P peh	Q kuh	R err	S ess	T the	U uh
ü uh umlaut	V fow	W veh	X iks	Y upsilon	Z tsett

Make sure you are familiar with the German alphabet, so that if a word is spelled out you know the letters.

Worked example

 LISTENING 6 · target C

Fill in the ID form for Alex.

First name: Alex
Surname: Schmidt
Age:
Date of birth:
Place of birth:
Postcode: D-

```
Frau: Wie heißen Sie?
Alex: Ich heiße Alex
Schmidt. S-C-H-M-I-D-T.
```

You have two chances to get this surname correctly. If you still miss a letter at the second hearing, make an intelligent guess!

EXAM ALERT!

If a word is spelled out on the recording, listen very carefully. It is important to spell the word 100% correctly.

Students have struggled with exam questions similar to this – **be prepared!** ResultsPlus

Listening tips

- You need to know the German question words (page 12). Even though exam paper questions are mostly in English, you may well hear questions in dialogues and interviews.
- The answers to listening questions always follow the order of questions on the paper, or as here, the headings on a form. So you won't hear the postcode until the end.

Now try this

 LISTENING 7 · target C

Listen to the rest of the recording and complete the ID form for Alex.

Countries

Learn countries and nationalities together. Many of them sound like English!

Länder

Upper case → ♂ ♀ ← Lower case

Country			Adjective
Deutschland	der Deutsche / ein Deutscher	die / eine Deutsche	deutsch
England	Engländer	Engländerin	englisch
Frankreich	Franzose	Französin	französisch
Großbritannien	Brite	Britin	britisch
Irland	Ire	Irin	irisch
Italien	Italiener	Italienerin	italienisch
Österreich	Österreicher	Österreicherin	österreichisch
Schottland	Schotte	Schottin	schottisch
Spanien	Spanier	Spanierin	spanisch
Wales	Waliser	Waliserin	walisisch
die Schweiz	Schweizer	Schweizerin	schweizerisch
die Türkei	Türke	Türkin	türkisch
die Vereinigten Staaten	Amerikaner	Amerikanerin	amerikanisch

Worked example

Write about where you and your family are from.

AIMING HIGHER

Obwohl ich Irin bin, habe ich nie in Irland gewohnt, weil ich in London geboren bin. Mein Vater ist Ire, aber meine Mutter kommt aus Südafrika. Sie haben sich an der Uni in London kennengelernt und nach dem Studium haben sie in der Hauptstadt Arbeit gefunden. Sie wollten nicht in ihre Heimatländer zurückkehren und deshalb wohnen wir in London, einer multikulturellen Stadt, die ich liebe.

Aiming higher

For a higher grade, try to include:
- a VARIETY of prepositions + correct endings
- a subordinating conjunction obwohl (although)
- er and sie forms, to allow for the use of ist (is) rather than bin (am)
- an imperfect modal verb Sie wollten nicht + negative
- confident control of word order shown by deshalb (therefore) + verb next.

Now try this

Write 60 words about where you come from.
- Welche Nationalität hast du? Und deine Eltern?
- Wo wurdest du geboren und wo wohnst du jetzt?

Use the **past** tense to describe where you were born, then the **present** for where you live now.

Brothers and sisters

This page will help you to say lots about your brothers and sisters, even if you don't get on!

Geschwister

Geschwister (npl)	siblings
Zwillinge (mpl)	twins
Mein Bruder nervt mich.	My brother annoys me.
Wir streiten uns ständig.	We argue constantly.
Ich bin ein Einzelkind.	I am an only child.

Ich komme schlecht mit meinem Bruder aus.
I get on badly with my brother.

Ich kann meine Schwester nicht ausstehen.
I can't stand my sister.

Ich verstehe mich gut mit meiner Schwester.
I get on well with my sister.

Ich habe meinen Bruder sehr gern.
I really like my brother.

Bei uns gibt es immer Streit.
We are always having rows.

Ich habe eine Stiefschwester, die Rosa heißt.
I have a stepsister, who is called Rosa.

Ich kann meine Halbschwester nicht leiden.
I can't stand my half-sister.

The verb haben (to have)
Present tense

ich	habe	I have
du	hast	you have
er / sie / es	hat	he / she / it has
wir	haben	we have
ihr	habt	you have
Sie / sie	haben	you / they have

Imperfect tense
ich hatte (I had)
wir hatten (we had)

Perfect tense
ich habe / er hat ... gehabt
(I have / he has ... had)

Vary the tense of haben to improve your sentences:

Als Kind habe ich mich oft mit meinem Bruder gestritten. As a child, I often argued with my brother.

Worked example

Read the text.

Ich komme sehr gut mit meinem ältesten Bruder aus. Er ist 18 Jahre alt und sehr lustig. Mit meiner jüngeren Schwester habe ich nichts gemeinsam – sie liebt Pferde und ich bevorzuge Rockmusik und Skateboarden.

Kathrin, 16

How old is Kathrin's sister?
(a) 18   (b) 13   (c) 16

- Don't ignore **titles** and **captions** – here, the caption giving Kathrin's age is crucial to answering the question.
- The answer is not spelled out in words such as 'My sister is 13 years old', but if you underline the key words (Schwester and jüngeren) and read the caption telling you that Kathrin is 16 you are on your way to the answer.
- So, if Kathrin is 16, you can cross out (c) as the answer because her sister is 'younger' than her, so she must be (b) 13, as that is the only age younger than 16.

Now try this

Adapt the sentences above to help you.

Give an introduction to your brothers and sisters in about 100 words.

Family

Include details of your family in any topic. It's crucial vocabulary to know and use.

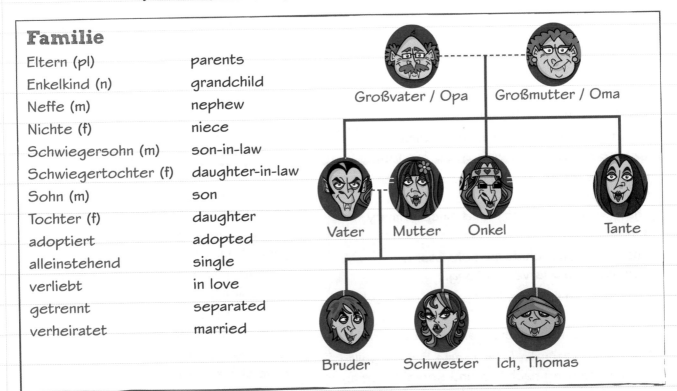

Familie

Eltern (pl)	parents
Enkelkind (n)	grandchild
Neffe (m)	nephew
Nichte (f)	niece
Schwiegersohn (m)	son-in-law
Schwiegertochter (f)	daughter-in-law
Sohn (m)	son
Tochter (f)	daughter
adoptiert	adopted
alleinstehend	single
verliebt	in love
getrennt	separated
verheiratet	married

Großvater / Opa Großmutter / Oma

Vater Mutter Onkel Tante

Bruder Schwester Ich, Thomas

Worked example

Was machst du am Wochenende mit deiner Familie?

AIMING HIGHER In meiner Familie ist es eine Tradition, uns jedes Wochenende zusammen einen Fernsehfilm anzusehen. Wir machen dies bereits seit meiner Kindheit und nächstes Wochenende werden wir wieder zusammen auf dem Sofa sitzen und einen gemütlichen Familienabend genießen.

Aiming higher

Use different tenses to talk about your family:

- a special family event in the PAST
- a regular happening in the PRESENT, such as a visit to an elderly relative
- FUTURE family plans
- the sort of family you would rather have using the CONDITIONAL tense
- seit + PRESENT tense:

Wir streiten uns schon seit vier Tagen.

We have been arguing for four days.

Using a funny family photo as a starting point in your speaking assessment can help a lot – a bit of humour cheers thing up and helps make you feel relaxed ... and more confident.

Now try this

Describe a family activity, in 6–8 sentences.

Use the advice above to help you include different tenses.

Friends

Are friends the new family? Look at this page to help you give your opinion.

Freunde

Freunde finde ich sehr wichtig.
I find friends very important.

Wir kommen gut miteinander aus.
We get on well with each other.

Mit guten Freunden ist man nie einsam.
You are never lonely with good friends.

Ich kenne meine beste Freundin seit der Grundschule.
I have known my best friend since primary school.

Unsere Freundschaft ist sehr stark.
Our friendship is very strong.

Es ist mir egal, ob meine Freunde reich oder arm sind.
I don't care if my friends are rich or poor.

Die ideale Freundin / Der ideale Freund sollte meiner Meinung nach lieb und sportlich sein.
The ideal friend, in my opinion, should be kind and sporty.

Using sollen (should be)

sollen + infinitive

ich sollte	wir sollten
du solltest	ihr solltet
er / sie sollte	Sie / sie sollten

Ein guter Freund sollte treu sein.
A good friend should be loyal.

Ein guter Freund sollte …
A good (male) friend should …

Eine gute Freundin sollte …
A good (female) friend should …

… geduldig sein.
… be patient.

… immer Zeit für mich haben.
… always have time for me

… dieselben Interessen wie ich haben.
… have the same interests.

… nie schlechter Laune sein.
… never be in a bad mood.

… immer guter Laune sein.
… always be in a good mood.

Grammar page 100

Worked example

Describe your best friend.

Mein bester Freund hat vier Beine und heißt Rex – das ist mein Hund! Er ist lustig und sehr lebhaft. Wir kommen gut miteinander aus. Mit ihm bin ich nie einsam.

AIMING HIGHER
Mein bester Freund hatte vier Beine und er war lustig und sehr lebhaft. Wir sind prima miteinander ausgekommen, aber leider ist er vor Kurzem gestorben, also habe ich jetzt keinen besten Freund mehr. Ohne ihn finde ich das Leben einsam. Bald werde ich hoffentlich einen neuen Hund bekommen.

- Add something **unusual** or **quirky** to your work. This student decided to talk about his dog being his best friend, which gives a refreshing approach.
- To improve his writing, this student could have adapted the text slightly to include **more than one** tense.

This second student is writing at a higher level due to her secure use of a **variety** of tenses: imperfect, perfect, present and future.

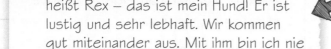

Now try this

Think of an 'unusual' best friend to answer these questions about, in about 100 words.

- Wer ist dein bester Freund / deine beste Freundin?
- Welche Charaktereigenschaften hat er / sie?
- Warum magst du ihn / sie?

Ich mag ihn / sie, weil + verb to the end.

Sie / Er ist + qualifier (ziemlich / äußerst) + adjective (süß / freundlich).

General hobbies

Make sure you have plenty of ideas on leisure time activities to talk about.

Hobbys

 Ich sehe gern fern.

 Ich spiele gern Computerspiele.

 Ich höre gern Musik.

 Ich koche gern.

 Ich lese gern.

 Ich spiele gern Schach.

 Ich verschicke gern SMS.

 Ich gehe gern kegeln.

Present tense (regular)

Grammar page 97

machen – to do / to make

ich	mache
du	machst	← infinitive
er / sie / es	macht
wir	machen
ihr	macht
Sie / sie	machen

Gehen (to go) follows the same pattern as machen in the present tense.

 Ich mache Fitnesstraining. I do training

 Ich gehe gern aus. I like going out.

Worked example

LISTENING 8 **target E**

What does Anna enjoy doing in her free time? Put a cross in the correct box.

(a) Shopping ☐
(b) Cooking ☒
(c) Going out ☐

– In meiner Freizeit bin ich meistens in der Küche zu finden, weil ich sehr gern backe.

- You are not necessarily going to hear the **exact** phrase you are familiar with, but you will hear enough to lead you to the words you know.
- Anna says she is mostly **in der Küche**. **Küche** = kitchen, so select the phrase which is related to this.
- There is only one suitable answer here, which is (b) Cooking. Nothing else is vaguely related to 'kitchen' or 'baking'.

Now try this

LISTENING 9 **target E**

Listen to the rest of the recording. Put a cross in the correct box for these three people's hobbies.

1 (a) Computer games ☐   (b) Television ☐   (c) Cycling ☐

2 (a) Music ☐   (b) Walking ☐   (c) Bowling ☐

3 (a) Sport ☐   (b) Cinema ☐   (c) Reading ☐

Don't miss the negative **nicht** for the third speaker.

Sports

You may want to refer to sports when talking about various topics. Make sure the main VERB always comes in SECOND position in a sentence.

Sportarten

ich ...	I ...
angle	go fishing
jogge	jog
reite	ride / go riding
fahre Rad	go cycling
fahre Skateboard	go skateboarding
gehe schwimmen	go swimming
mache Gymnastik	do gymnastics
mache Leichtathletik	do athletics
laufe Rollschuh	go roller skating
spiele Fußball	play football
spiele Tischtennis	play table tennis
treibe Sport	do sport

Ich bin Mitglied einer Hockeymannschaft.
I am a member of a hockey club.
Letzte Saison haben wir die Meisterschaft gewonnen.
We won the championship last season.

Verb in second place

Grammar page 94

1 Ich **2** spiele **3** Rugby.

1 Im Winter **2** spiele **3** ich Rugby.

In the perfect tense, the part of haben or sein goes in second place.

1 Im Winter **2** habe **3** ich Rugby **4** gespielt.

Im Sommer spiele ich Tennis.

Worked example

SPEAKING

Welche Sportarten treibst du?

AIMING HIGHER Ich bin sehr aktiv und treibe dreimal in der Woche Sport. Letztes Jahr war es ganz anders, weil ich mir das Bein gebrochen hatte und vier Monate lang keinen Sport treiben konnte. Das war eine Katastrophe für mich und ich musste dauernd Computerspiele spielen, die ich langweilig fand. Mein Traum ist es, eines Tages Profifußballspieler zu werden und ich würde am allerliebsten für Chelsea spielen.

Aiming higher

Including three tenses in your work is as easy as ... 1, 2, 3, if you can say which sports you:

- DO now
- DID previously
- WOULD LIKE or WILL do.

Use past tense 'markers' such as **letztes Jahr** (last year), **in der vorigen Saison** (last season), **als Kind** (as a child), **vor einigen Monaten** (a few months ago).

Now try this

SPEAKING

Answer these three questions.

1 Wie viel Sport treibst du jetzt?
2 Wie viel Sport hast du letztes Jahr gemacht?
3 Was wäre dein sportlicher Traum?

Here's a useful higher level phrase:
Mein Traum ist es, mein Land bei den Olympischen Spielen zu vertreten. It is my dream to represent my country at the Olympic Games.

Arranging to go out

Sie or du? If you are ever unsure, use Sie until the other person suggests using du.

Mit Freunden ausgehen

Möchtest du ...   Would you like to ...
  einen Film sehen?   see a film?
  schwimmen gehen?   go swimming?
  zur Hochzeit /   come to the wedding /
  Taufe kommen?   christening?
  zu meiner   come to my
  Geburtstagsfeier   birthday party?
  kommen?
Ich würde lieber ...   I would prefer to ...
  in den Jugendklub   go to the youth club.
  gehen.
  im Skatepark   hang out at the
  herumhängen.   skate park.
  zu Hause chillen.   chill at home.
Hast du am Samstag frei?
Are you free on Saturday?
Gehst du lieber ins Kino oder ins Konzert?
Do you prefer going to the cinema or to a concert?
Kaufst du die Eintrittskarten?
Are you buying the tickets?
Wann beginnt die Vorstellung?
When does the performance start?

weil (because)

Grammar page 95

weil ALWAYS sends the verb to the END.

Ich kann nicht kommen, weil ...
I can't come because ...

ich dann Fußballtraining mache.
I've got football training then.

ich kein Geld habe.
I haven't got any money.

meine Eltern es nicht erlauben.
my parents won't allow it.

Verwandte zu Besuch sind.
relatives are visiting.

> Haben and sein in the perfect tense go after the participle.
> Modal verbs go after the infinitive.

Ich kann nicht kommen, weil ...
I can't come because ...

... ich den Film schon gesehen habe.
... I have already seen the film.

... ich Hausaufgaben machen muss.
... I've got to do homework.

Worked example

Listen to the conversation and complete the two sentences with English words.

Anna is invited to the ... *cinema*.

She can't go, as she has to ... *go to tennis training*.

– Hallo Anna! Wir gehen heute Abend ins Kino. Möchtest du mitkommen?

– Oh nein, ich kann nicht kommen, weil ich dann Tennistraining mache.

Learning vocabulary

To prepare for listening exams, you need to learn lots of vocabulary.

- LOOK at and learn the words.
- COVER the English words.
- WRITE the English words.
- LOOK at all the words.
- SEE how many you have got right.

For an extra challenge, cover the GERMAN words and repeat the above stages.

Now try this

Listen to the rest of the recording and complete the sentences with the words or phrases in the box.

| the sports centre | the restaurant | the swimming pool |
| to do homework | to look after someone | no money |

1 Thomas is invited to go to ....

2 He can't go, as he has ....

3 Sara is invited to go to ....

4 She can't go, as she has ....

Last weekend

Use this page to learn some key past tense phrases to use in your speaking and writing assessments.

Letztes Wochenende

Ich bin zu Hause geblieben.	I stayed at home.
Ich bin ins Kino gegangen.	I went to the cinema.
Ich bin in die Disko gegangen.	I went to the disco.
Ich war im Jugendklub.	I was at the youth club.
Ich habe Verwandte besucht.	I visited relatives.
Ich habe mich gut amüsiert.	I had a good time.
Ich habe mich gelangweilt.	I was bored.
Ich habe nichts Besonderes gemacht.	I didn't do anything special.
Ich habe mich ausgeruht.	I relaxed.

Question words Grammar page 108

Wann?	When?
Warum?	Why?
Was?	What?
Wer?	Who?
Wie?	How?
Wo?	Where?
Was für ...?	What sort of?
Wen? Wem?	Who(m)?
Wessen?	Whose?
Wie viele?	How many?

Ich war auf einer Feier.
I was at a party.

Worked example

What did Lena do last weekend and what are her plans for next weekend?

(a) Reading   (d) Walking
(b) Shopping   (e) Music
(c) Going to a party (f) Ice skating

	Last weekend	Next weekend
Example:	b ☐ ☐	☐ ☐

– Hast du ein schönes Wochenende gehabt, Lena?

– Ja, ziemlich. Letzten Samstag habe ich im Schlussverkauf eine Jeans zum halben Preis gekauft.

EXAM ALERT!

Many students did quite well in this question but the concept of past and future leisure activities caused difficulty for some.

For 'last weekend' activities you need to listen for words in the past tense (**war**, past participles).

For 'next weekend' you need future tense or present tenses + future intention phrases – **habe ... vor** (intend to), **vielleicht** (perhaps) and **nächstes Wochenende** (next weekend).

> This was a real exam question that a lot of students struggled with – **be prepared!**   ResultsPlus

Now try this

Listen to the rest of the recording and complete the activity above in the worked example.

ein Roman (m) = ein Buch (n)

TV programmes

When reading or listening to passages about TV programmes, time phrases such as those below can all help you identify the tense.

Fernsehsendungen

Ich sehe mir gern ... an.	I like watching ...
die Nachrichten (fpl)	the news
die Tagesschau	the news (of ARD)
Dokumentarfilme (mpl)	documentaries
Quizsendungen (fpl)	quiz programmes
Seifenopern (fpl)	soap operas
Sendungen (fpl) / Programme (npl)	(TV) programmes
Serien (fpl)	series
Zeichentrickfilme (mpl)	cartoons
einschalten	to switch on
ausschalten	to switch off
Fernsehstar (m)	TV celebrity
Kabelfernsehen (n)	cable TV
Lieblings-	favourite
Zuschauer (m)	viewer

ZDF and ARD are TV broadcasters.

Tense markers

Past tense

als kleines Kind	as a small child
früher	previously, in the past
gestern	yesterday
letzte Woche	last week

Present tense

heute	today
heutzutage	these days
jetzt	now
normalerweise	normally

Future tense

in Zukunft	in future
morgen (früh)	tomorrow (morning)
nächste Woche	next week
übermorgen	the day after tomorrow

Ich sehe mir gern Zeichentrickfilme an.

Worked example

Sophie is talking about TV programmes. Do the ones below belong in her past, present or future? Put a cross in the correct box.

	Past	Present	Future
(a) Music shows	☐	☒	☐
(b) Cartoons	☐	☐	☐
(c) Documentaries	☐	☐	☐
(d) The news	☐	☐	☐

– Normalerweise schalte ich nach der Schule immer den Fernseher ein und sehe mir eine Musiksendung an, weil ich ein Musikfan bin. Früher, als ich noch in der Grundschule war, habe ich mir immer Zeichentrickfilme angesehen. Das war immer ziemlich blöd, aber lustig.

- You are listening here for clues to the **tense**, not for opinions or whether Sophie watches these programmes or not.
- Big tense clues here are **normalerweise** (normally), **früher** (previously / in the past) and **war** (was).
- Not all past participles start with **ge-**. Separable verbs have the **ge-** nestling in the middle of the word so aren't that easy to spot, e.g. **angesehen** (watched).
- Don't assume **bin** (am) or **habe** (have) indicate present tense – check there is not a past participle, e.g. **angesehen, gekommen** to make it past not present tense.

Now try this

Listen to Sophie's full description to complete the activity above.

Cinema

Don't get bogged down in recounting every detail of a film – give a brief outline of the plot and then lots of opinions. You will need to use the imperfect tense.

Kino

Ich habe X im Kino / auf DVD gesehen.
I saw X at the cinema / on DVD.
Es war ein Abenteuerfilm / Gruselfilm / Liebesfilm.
It was an adventure / horror / love film.
Das Hauptthema war Liebe / Familie.
The main theme was love / family.
Die Atmosphäre war gruselig / blöd.
The atmosphere was creepy / silly.
Die Geschichte war kompliziert / romantisch.
The story was complicated / romantic.
Der Film spielte in Köln.
The film was set in Cologne.

mit Untertiteln	subtitled
synchronisiert	dubbed

Imperfect tense

ist	➡	war	(is / was)
hat	➡	hatte	(has / had)
geht	➡	ging	(goes / went)
spielt	➡	spielte	(plays / played)
fährt	➡	fuhr	(drive / drove)
kauft	➡	kaufte	(buys / bought)

Im Film ging es um Freiheit / einen Mord / ein Verhältnis.
The film was about freedom / a murder / a relationship.

Ich habe einen Horrorfilm gesehen.

Worked example WRITING

Describe a film you have seen recently.

AIMING HIGHER

Ich gehe ziemlich oft ins Kino, obwohl das sehr teuer ist. Manchmal lade ich einen Film aus dem Internet herunter, aber ich finde Filme auf der Breitwand im Kino viel spannender.
Der letzte Film, den ich mir angesehen habe, hieß „Am Waldrand". Es war ein Horrorfilm und er war sehr gruselig. Es ging um eine Clique, die in einem dunklen, alten Haus am Waldrand eine Geburtstagsparty feierte, aber jede Stunde ist irgendwie ein Jugendlicher verschwunden. Der Film war eigentlich ziemlich blöd und unglaubhaft, aber er war trotzdem unterhaltsam und die Spezialeffekte waren erstklassig.

irgendwie – somewhere
unglaubhaft – unbelievable
unterhaltsam – entertaining

Writing tips

- Make the description of the plot as CLEAR and CONCISE as possible; do not make it too complex.
- Avoid using lots of English film titles in your work – you are being assessed on your knowledge of German, not English.
- Make a PLAN for any writing you are preparing on a topic, even if it is just a small section of your overall piece.

General habits ➡ How often? ⤵
Title? ⬅ Specific film ⬅ Opinion?
⤷ Genre? ➡ Plot? ➡ Opinion?

This is an example of a good written answer because of the amount of complex information and structures present, including:
- a variety of tenses
- es ging um phrase
- a relative clause
- interesting vocabulary,

Now try this WRITING

Use the flowchart and the text above to describe a film you have seen recently. Write about 200 words.

Music

Whether you are never without your earphones or prefer to play in an orchestra, music is a good topic to include in your assessments.

Die Musik

Ich höre gern Popmusik.
I like listening to pop music.

Rapmusik / Rockmusik ist meine Lieblingsmusik.
Rap / rock is my favourite music.

Ich höre Musik auf meinem Handy.
I listen to music on my mobile phone.

Ich lade viel Musik aus dem Internet herunter.
I download a lot of music from the internet.

Ich gehe selten auf Konzerte.
I rarely go to concerts.

Ich höre gern Radio.
I like listening to the radio.

Die Tänzer waren einmalig. The dancers were amazing.

Favourite things

Use Lieblings- + any noun (lower case) to talk about favourite things.

-band / -gruppe (f) – group

-melodie (f) – tune

Lieblings-

-sänger m / -sängerin (f) – singer

-lied (n) – song

-orchester (n) – orchestra

Worked example

READING

target G-F

Match the labels to the instruments.

1 Ich spiele Flöte (c)   (a)
2 Ich spiele Geige (b)   (b)
3 Ich spiele Gitarre (f)   (c)
4 Ich spiele Klarinette (a) (d)
5 Ich spiele Klavier (g)   (e)
6 Ich spiele Schlagzeug (d) (f)
7 Ich spiele Trompete (e)   (g)

- Number 1 (**die Flöte**) is a cognate and is easy to match to the picture of a flute (c).
- Once you have matched that, you can go ahead and match the other cognates, which only leaves you with 2, 5 and 6.
- Number 6 (**das Schlagzeug**) you might be able to work out from **schlagen** (to hit) and **Zeug** (thing), i.e. a hitting thing = drum.
- And that just leaves you with Number 2 (**Geige**) and Number 5 (**Klavier**). One is a violin and one is a piano. But which is which?

Now try this

SPEAKING

Answer these questions.
- Was ist dein Lieblingslied?
- Warst du schon einmal auf einem Konzert?
- Wer ist dein(e) Lieblingssänger(in)?
- Wie sieht er / sie aus?

Was? – What? Wo? – Where?
Wer? – Who? Wie? – How?

Online activities

Use time phrases to add interest to your description of your online activities.

Aktivitäten online

Ich spiele online / Computerspiele.	I play online / computer games.
Ich lade Fotos hoch.	I upload photos.
Ich lade Musik herunter.	I download music.
Ich sehe mir Videoclips an.	I watch video clips.
Ich surfe im Internet.	I surf the internet.
Ich schreibe E-Mails / mein Blog.	I write emails / my blog.
Ich chatte online mit Freunden.	I chat to my friends online.
Ich besuche Chatrooms/benutze soziale Netzwerke.	I visit chatrooms / use social networking sites.
Ich skype.	I skype.
Ich schalte meinen Tablet-PC ein / aus.	I turn on / off my tablet.
Ich lese die Nachrichten am Computer.	I read the news on the computer.

dürfen (to be allowed to)

Grammar page 100

Dürfen is a modal verb so it needs an infinitive.

Ich darf nicht nach 22:00 Uhr auf Facebook surfen.
I am not allowed to be on Facebook after ten o'clock.

Ich darf keine Musik herunterladen.
I am not allowed to download music.

Worked example

LISTENING 16 — target A

Mia is talking about her evening activities at home. Answer the questions in English.

Why does Mia look forward to the evening?
Because she can relax.

— Ich freue mich immer auf den Abend, weil ich mich dann endlich einmal ausruhen darf.

Listening tips

- Don't worry about doing a simultaneous translation for yourself as you listen – read the questions in advance and then focus on the parts of the recording that are RELEVANT to those questions.

- The more practice you have of LISTENING to German, the easier you will find it. Make sure you listen to all the recorded material supplied with this Revision Guide to give your listening skills a boost.

Now try this

LISTENING 16 — target A

Listen and answer these questions to complete the above activity.

(a) Why does Mia watch the news?
(b) What does Mia do when she rings her friends?
(c) What does Mia upload?

 Make sure you note down the **adjective** that accompanies the noun here.

Daily routine

You will need to understand both the 12-hour and the 24-hour clock.

Mein Tagesablauf

Ich wache um sechs Uhr auf.	I wake up at 6 o'clock.
Zuerst bade / dusche ich.	First I have a bath / shower.
Dann ziehe ich mich an.	Then I get dressed
Ich schminke mich.	I put on my make-up.
Ich rasiere mich.	I shave.
Ich putze mir die Zähne.	I brush my teeth.
Ich bürste / kämme mir die Haare.	I brush / comb my hair.
Um zehn vor acht ...	At ten to eight ...
verlasse ich das Haus.	I leave home.
fahre ich mit dem Bus in die Schule.	I go by bus to school.
Um 16:00 Uhr kehre ich nach Hause zurück.	At 4 o'clock I return home.
Um 22:00 Uhr schlafe ich ein.	I fall asleep at 10 o'clock.

um – at
gegen – around

12-hour clock

 zwei Uhr

 fünf nach zwei

 Viertel nach zwei

 halb drei

Be careful! **Halb drei** is half-past two (literally, half **to** three).

 Viertel vor drei

 zehn vor drei

Worked example

Describe your daily routine.

> Normalerweise wache ich um halb sieben auf und ich dusche, bevor ich mich schminke und anziehe.

Make sure you include a conjunction such as **bevor** (before), which sends the verb to the end, to show a good command of German word order.

AIMING HIGHER

> Nachdem ich mich angezogen habe, frühstücke ich gegen sieben Uhr in der Küche. Dann putze ich mir die Zähne, bürste mir die Haare und schminke mich. Ich bin jetzt fertig und gehe mit meinem Freund, der in der Nähe wohnt, zur Schule.

- Raise your level by introducing the perfect tense after **nachdem** (after), plenty of accurate present tense verbs and round it all off with a relative pronoun clause.
- Show just how much you know by including a variety of grammatical constructions, **tenses** and **opinions** in your speaking assessment.

Adapt texts from this book to suit your writing and speaking assessments.

Now try this

Write a paragraph of 100 words to describe your daily routine once you come back from school.

Compare it to your weekend evening routine to give your answers more variety and depth.

Breakfast

Whether it's a full English or a grabbed bite from the corner shop on the way to school, breakfast is a good aspect of your daily routine to discuss.

Das Frühstück

Frühstück (n)	breakfast
frühstücken	to have breakfast
Bratwurst (f)	sausage
Brötchen (n) / Brot (n)	bread roll / bread
Ei (n)	egg
Rührei (n)	scrambled egg
Spiegelei (n)	fried egg
Frucht (f) / Obst (n)	fruit
Haferbrei (m)	porridge
Honig (m)	honey
Joghurt (m)	yoghurt
Marmelade (f)	jam
Müsli (n)	muesli
Toastbrot (n)	toast
eine Tasse Kaffee / Tee / Kakao	a cup of coffee / tea / cocoa
ein Glas Milch / Fruchtsaft	a glass of milk / fruit juice

Days of the week

am + days of the week

am Montag on Monday

Montag	Monday	Donnerstag	Thursday
Dienstag	Tuesday	Freitag	Friday
Mittwoch	Wednesday	Samstag / Sonnabend	Saturday
		Sonntag	Sunday

montags	on Mondays
am Montagvormittag / am Montagmorgen	on Monday morning
am Montagnachmittag	on Monday afternoon
am Montagabend	on Monday evening
Montagnacht	on Monday night

Worked example

Write about your breakfast on a Sunday.

Am Sonntag frühstücke ich oft erst um 13:00 Uhr, weil ich es so schwierig finde, aus dem Bett zu kommen! Am liebsten esse ich ein Spiegelei mit Toastbrot und Ketchup und ich trinke dazu eine große Tasse Kaffee.

AIMING HIGHER Nachdem ich gefrühstückt habe, setze ich mich vor den Fernseher und sehe mir die vielen Sendungen an, die ich während der Woche nicht gesehen habe. Das ist meine Lieblingsaktivität, aber leider muss ich danach Hausaufgaben machen. Das finde ich nicht so gut!

- Include more **complex language** by adding a day of the week + inversion so the verb remains in second place.
- Check **adjective endings** carefully in your grammar book to make sure you get them right.

- Aiming higher? Then add a relative pronoun + a past tense (die ich während der Woche nicht gesehen habe).
- And remember not to forget to include your opinion at the end.

Now try this

Write about 200 words to answer these questions.

- Was isst du normalerweise zum Frühstück?
- Was hast du letzten Sonntag zum Frühstück gegessen und getrunken?
- Wie wäre dein ideales Frühstück?

Eating at home

Make sure you know lots of food and drink vocabulary.

Zu Hause essen

Ich habe Hunger / Durst.	I am hungry / thirsty.	Salat (m)	salad
Ich bin satt.	I am full.	Schokolade (f)	chocolate
Mittagessen (n)	lunch	Suppe (f)	soup
Abendessen (n)	dinner	backen	to bake
Imbiss (m)	snack	braten	to roast, fry
Biokost (f)	organic food	grillen	to grill
Eis (n)	ice-cream	vorbereiten	to prepare
Fisch (m)	fish	fettig	greasy, fatty
Gemüse (n)	vegetables	fettarm	low-fat
Obst (n)	fruit	köstlich / lecker	delicious
Hähnchen (n)	chicken	roh	raw
Kartoffel (f)	potato	süß	sweet
Kotelett (n)	chop	scharf / würzig	spicy
Nudeln (fpl)	pasta		
Reis (m)	rice		

Opinions

Use schmecken to say if you do or don't like an item of food (literally 'It tastes to me good').

schmecken is followed by the dative case, so it needs mir.

Die Suppe schmeckt mir gut.
The soup tastes good.

Die Himbeeren schmecken mir nicht.
I don't like the raspberries.

Schmeckt dir das Hähnchen?
Do you like the chicken?

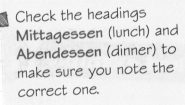

Worked example   target **D**

Read the text.

Mittagessen
Wir empfehlen gebackenen Fisch oder gegrilltes Hähnchen mit Reis oder Nudeln. Essen Sie doch mal Desserts mit frischem Obst und Vanilleeis oder Joghurt.

Abendessen
Essen Sie am Abend nur ein leichtes Essen, wie frisches Gemüse mit Dipp, Salat oder Suppe. Trinken Sie dazu Wasser, Kräutertee oder erfrischenden Fruchtsaft.

Is this item of food recommended for lunch, supper or neither?

Pasta lunch

Check the headings Mittagessen (lunch) and Abendessen (dinner) to make sure you note the correct one.

- Identify the German term for each food item (a)–(c) first.
- Look at **all** the words mentioned. You are not just looking for a 'chop', but for a 'grilled chop', so the accompanying adjective may be crucial to avoid making a mistake.

Now try this   target **D**

Look at the text above. Are these items of food recommended for lunch, supper or neither?

(a) Grilled chop   **(b)** Vegetables   **(c)** Soup

Healthy eating

Learn some of the phrases on this page so that you can talk about healthy eating.

Gesund essen

Normalerweise esse ich gesund.
I normally eat healthily.

Ich habe zugenommen.
I have put on weight.

Ich möchte ein Kilo abnehmen.
I would like to lose a kilo.

Fastfood schmeckt mir nicht mehr.
I no longer like fast food.

Ich esse zu viele Bonbons / Süßigkeiten.
I eat too many sweets.

Morgen mache ich Diät.
I am going on a diet tomorrow.

Die Fettleibigkeit breitet sich wie eine Epidemie aus.
Obesity is spreading like an epidemic.

Meine Tante ist an Krebs gestorben.
My aunt died of cancer.

Alkohol schädigt die Leber.
Alcohol damages the liver.

dünn / schlank	thin / slim
übergewichtig	overweight
(un)gesund	(un)healthy
vegetarisch	vegetarian

Three key tenses

To aim for grade C and above, you need to recognise these three tenses:

Past tense

- form of haben / sein + past participles
- als (when) usually indicates past tense
- watch out for imperfects war (was), hatte (had), es gab (there was/were)
- and pluperfect hatte gemacht (had done), war gefahren (had gone).

Present tense

- ends in -e for ich form and -t for er / sie form
- mind the irregulars: liest (reads), fährt (goes), isst (eats).

Watch out for present tense + future meaning:
Morgen esse ich gesund.
Tomorrow I am going to eat healthily.

Future tense

- form of werden (werde, wird) + infinitive;
- watch out for future conditionals würde (would) + infinitive and wäre (would be), möchte (would like) + infinitive.

Worked example

Listen. Do these activities belong to the past, present or future?

	Past	Present	Future
Eating fast food	☒	☐	☐

– Normalerweise esse ich gesund. Früher habe ich oft Fastfood gegessen, aber das schmeckt mir nicht mehr und seit einem Jahr bin ich Vegetarierin.

EXAM ALERT!

Many students find this type of task very challenging and score badly. You need to revise tenses carefully in order to be able to recognise different tenses in reading and listening passages.

Students have struggled with exam questions similar to this – be prepared!

ResultsPlus

Now try this

Listen to the rest of the recording. Do these activities belong to the past, present or future?

	Past	Present	Future
(a) Being vegetarian	☐	☐	☐
(b) Roller skating	☐	☐	☐
(c) Hiking	☐	☐	☐

Keeping fit

Learn some key phrases about keeping fit, even if you don't do it yourself!

Fit bleiben

Ich gehe oft ins Fitnesszentrum.	I often go to the gym.
Ich gehe joggen.	I go jogging.
Ich gehe regelmäßig laufen.	I run regularly.
Ich fahre Rad.	I cycle.
Ich treibe nie Sport.	I don't do any sport.
Ich trainiere täglich.	I exercise every day.
Ich halte mich fit.	I keep fit.
Ich entspanne mich beim Musikhören.	I relax by listening to music.
Ich leide unter Rückenschmerzen.	I suffer from backache.
Ich habe Atembeschwerden.	I have breathing difficulties.
Hallenbad (n)	indoor pool
Ruhe (f)	peace, calm
fit / nichtfit	fit / unfit
sportlich	sporty
müde	tired
nervös	nervous
schwindlig	dizzy
gestresst	stressed

Qualifiers

Add qualifiers to your adjectives whenever you can.

gar nicht	not at all
nicht	not
ein bisschen	a bit
ganz	quite
ziemlich	quite
meistens	mostly
sehr	very
besonders	especially
äußerst	extremely

Ich bin sehr sportlich.

You'll find plenty more sports vocabulary on page 10.

You'll find plenty more sports vocabulary on page 10.

Worked example

 SPEAKING

Was für einen Sport treibst du?

AIMING HIGHER Fußball ist mein Lieblingssport. Ich trainiere zweimal in der Woche mit meiner Mannschaft und sonntags spielen wir gegen andere Mannschaften. Gestern hatte ich eine Erkältung und ich konnte nicht trainieren, aber hoffentlich werde ich am Wochenende wieder fit sein.

Aiming higher

- Use past and future tenses to improve your answers, as here.
- Include a modal verb: ich konnte nicht trainieren.
- Add a more complex phrase: Je mehr wir trainieren, desto fitter und besser werden wir. The more we train, the fitter and better we become.

Now try this

 SPEAKING

Answer these questions.
- Welche Sportaktivitäten machst du?
- Wo machst du das?
- Wann machst du das?
- Wie entspannst du dich?

CONTROLLED ASSESSMENT

Remember to ask at least TWO of your own questions during the exam – interaction is what is wanted! Use the **Sie** (polite) form.

Treiben Sie gern Sport? Do you like doing sport?

Wie halten Sie sich fit? How do you keep fit?

Illness

Naming a body part and adding -schmerzen (pain) is an easy way to express where it hurts!

Krankheiten

Es geht mir gut / schlecht.	I'm well / ill.
Schmerz (m)	pain
Ich habe ...	I've got ...
Magenschmerzen (mpl)	stomach-ache
Bauchschmerzen (mpl)	stomach-ache
Halsschmerzen (mpl)	a sore throat
Kopfschmerzen (mpl)	a headache
Rückenschmerzen (mpl)	backache
Ich habe ...	
Durchfall (m)	diarrhoea
eine Erkältung (f) / einen Schnupfen (m)	a cold
Fieber (n)	temperature
Grippe (f)	the flu
Husten (n)	a cough
Ich bin / fühle mich krank.	I am/feel ill.
Mir ist übel.	I feel sick.

Saying something hurts

Mein(e) ... tut weh. My .... hurts.

Use tut (one thing) or tun (more than one thing) + weh.

⬇

Mein Fuß tut weh. My foot hurts.

⬇

Meine Füße tun weh. My feet hurt.

You can also talk about past pain:

Meine Hand tat weh. My hand hurt.

⬇

Meine Arme taten weh. My arms hurt.

Bein (n)	leg
Finger (m)	finger
Knie (n)	knee
Schulter (f)	shoulder

Worked example

Write about an accident.

AIMING HIGHER

Letztes Jahr konnte ich nicht in den Skiurlaub fahren, weil ich stattdessen mit gebrochenem Bein zu Hause bleiben musste. Es war ziemlich schade, denn drei Tage vor dem Urlaub bin ich beim Eishockeytraining total ausgerutscht. Ich wusste sofort, dass es schlimm war, weil ich nicht wieder aufstehen konnte. Ich wurde ins Krankenhaus gebracht, wo ich einen Gips bekam. Mensch, war das ein Pech!

Gips (m) – plaster cast

Aiming higher

Challenge yourself to include the following to achieve your best possible written work.

• Weil and dass clauses

• Dative prepositional phrases: mit gebrochenem Bein (with a broken leg), beim Eishockeytraining (at ice hockey training)

• Correct word order: TIME, MANNER, PLACE

• Modal verbs in the imperfect: konnte, musste, wusste

• Idioms: es war schade (it was a shame / pity), Pech (bad luck)

Now try this

Can you tell the story behind this picture? Write about 200 words.

Look back at the bullet points above and include as many elements as possible in your writing.

Health problems

Alcohol, drugs and smoking are the focus here. This vocabulary is mainly for Higher level students who want to cover these issues in the assessments.

Grammar page 97

Gesundheitsprobleme

Alkohol (m)	alcohol
alkoholfrei	non-alcoholic
alkoholisch	alcoholic
betrunken	drunk
Entziehungskur (f)	rehab
Gewohnheit (f)	habit
Sucht (f)	addiction
Droge (f)	drug
rauchen	to smoke
Raucher (m)	smoker
Rauschgift (n)	drug
Tabak (m)	tobacco
Tablette (f)	tablet, pill
Zigarette (f)	cigarette
abhängig	dependent
aufhören	to stop
bewusstlos	unconscious
probieren	to try
schädlich	harmful
spritzen	to inject

Present tense irregulars

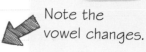

Note the vowel changes.

aufgeben – to give up		nehmen – to take	
ich	gebe ... auf	ich	nehme
du	gibst	du	nimmst
er / sie / es	gibt	er / sie / es	nimmt
wir	geben	wir	nehmen
ihr	gebt	ihr	nehmt
Sie/sie	geben	Sie/sie	nehmen

Learning vocabulary

Look at the 'word family' for Alkohol.

alkoholfrei
alcohol-free

alkoholisch
alcoholic

Alkohol (m)
alcohol

alkoholsüchtig
addicted to
alcohol

Alkoholiker/in (m/f)
an alcoholic

alkoholarm
low in alcohol

Worked example

LISTENING 19   target A

Lukas is talking about his health.

Put a cross in the box under the person the statement refers to.

	Lukas	Susanne	Grandad
I can't stop smoking.	X		

– Ich rauche seit fünf Jahren. Es ist zu einer schlimmen Gewohnheit geworden und ich habe oft versucht, aufzugeben, aber ich habe es nie geschafft. Sobald jemand mir eine Zigarette reicht ... na ich fange wieder an.

- Read the **title** and the **rubric** before you listen – here you can get one step ahead by knowing the extract is going to be on the subject of habits and health, and involves three characters.

- The start of the text is all in the 'I' form, **ich**, and you already know that Lukas is doing the talking, so the statement refers to himself.

Now try this

LISTENING 20   target A

Listen to the whole extract. Who does each statement refer to: Lukas, Susanne or Grandad?

(a) I am often ill.

(b) I think cigarettes are damaging my health.

(c) I am totally against smoking.

(d) I will never smoke in front of my family.

At the tourist office

You may want to talk about visitor attractions in your speaking assessment. The 24-hour clock is used a lot in Germany, so check you are confident using it.

Beim Verkehrsamt

besuchen/besichtigen	to visit
stattfinden	to take place
Auskunft (f)	information
Broschüre (f)	brochure
Touristeninformation (f)	tourist information
Unterhaltungsmöglichkeiten (fpl) things to do	

Die Rundfahrt beginnt pünktlich um acht Uhr.
The tour begins at eight o'clock prompt.

Der Ausflug findet am Dienstag statt.
The trip takes place on Tuesday.

Der Eintritt / Eintrittspreis ist €6.
Entry is €6.

Es gibt eine Studentenermäßigung.
There is a student discount.

Die Öffnungszeiten sind täglich von neun bis sechzehn Uhr.
The opening times are daily from nine until four o'clock.

24-hour clock

The 24-hour clock is easy if you know your numbers.

It is used for opening times, train times or to say when an event is taking place.

 neun Uhr dreißig

 zwölf Uhr fünfundvierzig

 sechzehn Uhr fünfzehn

 zwanzig Uhr vierzig

 dreiundzwanzig Uhr

---

Worked example SPEAKING

Read the information at the tourist office and tell a visitor what they could do in this town.

- **Kunstgalerie, 10:00–15:30 Uhr, montags geschlossen**
- **Ausflug nach Salzburg, Sonntag, 10:00 Uhr**
- **Stadtrundgang, Donnerstag, 13:00 Uhr**
- **Stadtmuseum, dienstags–samstags, 9:30–17:00 Uhr geöffnet**

AIMING HIGHER

Try to add adjectives – the simple addition of **gut** + ending in **eine gute Kunstgalerie** shows you know how to handle German grammar.

Es gibt eine gute Kunstgalerie, aber am Montag ist sie geschlossen. Ich gehe oft dahin, weil Kunst mein Lieblingsfach ist.

Montags kann man leider nicht in die Kunstgalerie gehen, weil sie geschlossen ist, aber sonst kann man von 10:00 bis 15:30 Uhr dahin gehen. Die Ausstellungen dort sind großartig, und die Ermäßigung für Studenten und Senioren ist hervorragend.

Pay attention to words such as **geöffnet** (open) and **geschlossen** (closed) so you give the correct information.

Using **großartig** (great) and **hervorragend** (outstanding) makes a refreshing change from the overused **toll**, **klasse** or **super**.

Now try this SPEAKING

Talk for one minute about three more things you can do in the above town, giving as many details as possible.

Out and about

What to do in town

This page will give you lots of useful phrases for describing activites in your town.

Was kann man in der Stadt machen?

Man kann …	You can …
einen Spaziergang machen	go for a walk
einen Rundgang machen	go on a tour
die Sehenswürdigkeiten besuchen	visit the sights
Fotos machen	take photos
Postkarten schicken	send postcards
bummeln (gehen)	stroll around
einkaufen gehen	go shopping
schwimmen gehen	go swimming
ins Kino gehen	go to the cinema
tanzen gehen	go dancing
im Café essen	eat in a café
sich gut amüsieren	have a good time
sich mit Freunden treffen	meet friends

Negatives

If you want to say what you CAN'T do, use kein (not a / no) with an article or nicht (not) with a verb.

Man kann keinen Spaziergang machen, weil es hier zu viel Verkehr gibt. You can't go for a walk because there is too much traffic here.

Hier kann man nicht ins Kino gehen, weil es seit einem Jahr geschlossen ist. You can't go to the cinema here because it has been shut for a year.

Worked example

LISTENING 21 · target C

What can Karl do in his town? Put a cross in the correct box.

	Karl	Nina
(a) Shopping	☐	☐
(b) Swimming	☒	☐
(c) Meet friends	☐	☐
(d) Wander round	☐	☐
(e) Go to the cinema	☐	☐

– Hallo, ich heiße Karl und ich wohne in einer kleinen Stadt in Süddeutschland. Im Sommer ist es toll, weil man schwimmen gehen und den ganzen Tag draußen im Wasser verbringen kann.

Careful listening

- Listen really carefully and don't jump to conclusions!
- Use the second listening to double-check you haven't missed anything, such as an important negative.

- Look at how Karl describes his town to give you ideas for describing your town.
- Karl mentions **Geschäfte** and **Kinos**, but don't miss the important **k-** before **eine** which makes the negative **keine** – there are **no** shops or cinemas where he lives.

Now try this

LISTENING 22 · target C

What can Karl and Nina do in their town? Listen to the rest of the recording and put a cross in the correct box for either Karl or Nina in the above exercise.

Read this question really carefully – it is asking what Karl and Nina **can** do in their town, not what they **can't** do.

Signs around town

Signs in a town can sometimes be tricky – you need to read them carefully.

Schilder in der Stadt

(Bus)Bahnhof (m)	(bus) station
Abfall / Müll (m)	rubbish
Ausgang (m)	exit
drücken / ziehen	push / pull
Eingang (m)	entrance
Geldautomat (m)	cashpoint
Schnellimbiss (m)	snack bar
Stadtzentrum (n)	town centre
Toiletten (fpl) / WC (n)	toilets
Veranstaltung (f)	event

Notausgang   Emergency exit

Parken verboten   No parking

Herzlich Willkommen   Welcome

Negative words

Signs with these words on are warnings NOT to do something!

(**nicht**)   (**kein**)   (**verboten**)   (**Achtung**)

not   not a / no   forbidden   Attention!

 Bitte hier nicht rauchen

 Schwimmen verboten

Worked example

READING **target E**

Read these signs. Decide who should have read each one.

1. Bitte Schuhe ausziehen

2. Hier ist Rauchen streng verboten   (a)

3. Haustiere sind in unserem Haus immer willkommen

(a) Kerem is having a cigarette.
(b) Lara has left her dog tied up outside.
(c) Georg has footwear on.

Reading tips

- You don't need to understand every word to answer this question. Just find the LINKS and you will have the answer.

- This reading question has very few words – but you still need to concentrate to avoid making careless mistakes.

Link key words to help you find the answers:
Schuhe = shoes, so links to footwear
Rauchen = smoking, so links to cigarette
Haustiere = pets, so links to dog

Now try this

READING **target E**

Complete the rest of the activity above, then try the question below.

Who has read this sign?   **Tür nicht drücken, Tür nicht ziehen – bitte links klingeln!**

(a) Kerem is pushing the door.
(b) Georg is ringing the bell.
(c) Lara is pulling the door.

At the station

You may meet station vocabulary in listening and reading texts, so it's well worth learning it.

Am Bahnhof

Abfahrt (f)	departure
Abteil (n)	compartment
Ankunft (f)	arrival
Busbahnhof (m)	bus station
Bushaltestelle (f)	bus stop
mit dem Bus	by bus
den Zug verpassen	to miss a train
Fahrer (m)	driver
Fahrkarte / Karte (f)	ticket
Fahrkartenautomat (m)	ticket machine
Fahrkartenschalter (m)	ticket counter
Fahrplan (m)	timetable
Gepäckaufbewahrung (f)	left luggage
Gleis (n)	platform
Schlafwagen (m)	sleeping carriage
Verspätung (f)	delay
Wartesaal (m)	waiting room

Separable verbs

Grammar page 98

Separable verbs break into two parts:
- main verb = second in the sentence
- prefix = at the end.

Make sure you can use separable verbs in all tenses.

umsteigen – to change (trains)

Present	Ich steige in Ulm um.
Past	Ich bin in Ulm umgestiegen.
Future	Ich werde in Ulm umsteigen.
Modals	Ich muss in Ulm umsteigen.

More separable verbs

einsteigen	to get on, board
aussteigen	to get off
abfahren	to depart
ankommen	to arrive

Worked example

Listen and complete the grid.

	Single →	Return ↔	Depart	Arrive
1		X	7:30	8:40
2				
3				
4				

- Ich möchte bitte nach Bremen fahren.
- Einfach oder hin und zurück?
- Hin und zurück, bitte. Wann fährt der nächste Zug ab?
- Er fährt um sieben Uhr dreißig ab und er kommt um acht Uhr vierzig in Bremen an.

EXAM ALERT!

Although this is not a particularly high-level task, most students find listening for times really difficult, so it's worth practising them.

Look at the answer grid before you listen, so you know what sort of information you need to focus on.

> Students have struggled with exam questions similar to this – **be prepared!**
> ResultsPlus

- Don't make careless mistakes by confusing **vierzig** (40) with **vierzehn** (14), etc.
- The person asks for **hin und zurück** (return). He could also have said **einfach** (one way).
- Listen carefully for separable verbs like **abfahren** – ab might have split from fahren, so listen to the whole sentence to check the time relates to a departure time, not an arrival.

Now try this

Listen to three more dialogues at the train station and complete the grid above.

Weather

There are lots of cognates in weather vocabulary, so it shouldn't take you long to master these.

Das Wetter

 Es ist sonnig.   Es ist kalt.   Es ist neblig.

 Es ist windig.   Es ist heiß.   Es schneit.

 Es ist bewölkt / wolkig.   Es regnet.   Es donnert und blitzt.

Es friert	It's freezing
Es hagelt	It's hailing
Jahreszeit (f)	season
im Frühling	in spring
im Sommer	in summer
im Herbst	in autumn
im Winter	in winter

Weather in different tenses

Add value to these weather expressions by adapting them to different tenses.

PRESENT Es regnet. It is raining.

IMPERFECT Es war regnerisch/Es regnete. It was rainy / raining.

PERFECT Es hat geregnet. It rained.

PLUPERFECT Es hatte geregnet. It had rained.

FUTURE Es wird regnen. It will rain.

More weather words to try out in different tenses:

Es ist / war / wird ... sein.	It is / was / will be ...
bedeckt	overcast
heiter	bright
frostig	frosty
nass	wet
schlecht	bad
trocken	dry

Worked example

Read the weather forecast.

> Nach Osten hin wird der Wind am Dienstag immer schwächer werden. Höchstwerte liegen bei –14 Grad am Alpenrand und bis –1 Grad an der Ostseeküste. Die Nacht über wird es stark schneien. Es bleibt weiterhin bedeckt.

What sort of weather is heading for this area?

(a) Sunshine ☐
(b) Snow ☒
(c) Strong winds ☐

EXAM ALERT!

Some students struggle with multiple-choice as they jump to the wrong conclusion. It is the **detail** that you have to look out for. In this text, strong winds is option (c) but weaker winds are mentioned in the text, so (c) can't be right.

Students have struggled with exam questions similar to this – **be prepared!** Results

- Read to the very end of the report to find the word **bedeckt** (cloudy), so you can rule out (a) Sunshine.
- The minus temperatures and the verb **schneien** (to snow) in the future tense tell you that snow is on its way – answer (b).

Now try this

Complete these questions on the text above.

1 The wind: (a) got stronger yesterday. ☐
   (b) will lessen on Tuesday. ☐
   (c) will get worse on Tuesday. ☐

2 The Alps: (a) will be colder than the coast. ☐
   (b) will be warmer than the coast. ☐
   (c) will see a lot of rain. ☐

Places in town

Places in town may be familiar but check details such as spelling and gender carefully.

In der Stadt

Bibliothek (f)	library
Bowling (n)	bowling
Einkaufszentrum (n)	shopping centre
Eishalle (f)	ice rink
Flohmarkt (m)	flea market
Freizeitzentrum (n)	leisure centre
Geschäft (n) / Laden (m)	shop
Hallenbad (n)	indoor pool
Kino (n)	cinema
Kirche (n)	church
Kneipe (f) / Lokal (n)	pub
Museum (n)	museum
Nachtklub (m)	nightclub
Spielplatz (m)	playground
Sportzentrum (n)	sports centre
Theater (n)	theatre

Es gibt ... (there is / are ...)

Use es gibt + accusative (einen, eine, ein) in different tenses to help improve your speaking and writing.

PRESENT Es gibt ... There is ...

IMPERFECT Als ich klein war, gab es ... When I was young, there was ...

PLUPERFECT Vorher hatte es ... gegeben. Earlier there had been ...

FUTURE In Zukunft wird es ... geben. In future there will be ...

CONDITIONAL In meiner idealen Stadt gäbe es ... In my ideal town there would be ...

... eine Eishalle

Adjectives

Make sure you have a good supply of adjectives to express your opinion.

😊

| großartig | magnificent | sauber | clean |
| hübsch | pretty | malerisch | picturesque |

🙁

| dreckig / schmutzig | dirty |
| hässlich | ugly |

😐

| klein | small |
| ruhig | quiet |

Worked example

Is this town good for young people?

Für Sportler:	Freizeitzentrum mit Hallenbad
Für Filmfans:	modernes Kino mit den neuesten Kinohits
Für Kulturfreunde:	historische Kirche in der Stadtmitte
Für Teenager:	Tanzen in Nachtklubs
Für Familien:	großartige Spielplätze und Skateparks

Put a cross by one facility mentioned.

Theatre ☐
Cinema ☐
Shopping ☐
Football ☐
Church ☐
Swimming ☒
Zoo ☐
Dancing ☐
Rollerblading ☐

Look at the words in the question and then scan the text to see if you can find any immediate matches. You may recognise **Hallenbad** in the first part of the text, which means 'indoor swimming pool', so you can put a cross by 'swimming'.

Now try this

What else can you do in the above town? Put a cross by **four** more facilities.

Around town

When you talk about places, try to include some comparisons, to help you aim higher.

In der Stadt

Dom (m)	cathedral
Gebäude (n)	building
Fabrik (f)	factory
Grünanlage (f) / Park (m)	park / open space
Informationsbüro (n)	information office
Markt / Marktplatz (m)	market
Rathaus (n)	town hall
Schloss (n)	castle
Stadtteil (m)	part of town
Stadtviertel (n)	district of town
Verkehrsamt (n)	tourist office

Comparisons

Grammar page 92

Make your writing more interesting by using COMPARATIVES and SUPERLATIVES.

Meine Stadt ist ... / My town is ...	interessant. / interesting.
	interessanter als Hamburg. / more interesting than Hamburg.
	am interessantesten. / most interesting.
	eine der interessantesten Städte in Deutschland. / one of the most interesting towns in Germany.

Meine Stadt hat viele Grünanlagen.

Meine Stadt ist interessanter als deine Stadt.

Worked example

Read this tourist information.

Entdecken Sie Rothenburg – die schönste Stadt Deutschlands

Rothenburg ist eines der beliebtesten Touristenziele in Deutschland. Die kleine Stadt hat viele historische Gebäude, wie das Rathaus und das Burgtor, das zu den ältesten Gebäuden der Stadt zählt. Weitere Informationen findet man beim Verkehrsamt in der Innenstadt. Gehen Sie dorthin, um die günstigsten Theaterkarten zu reservieren.

- Look for the key words **reservieren** and **Theaterkarten**. Then go back to discover you can buy them at the **Verkehrsamt** (tourist office).
- It doesn't matter if you don't understand words like **günstigsten** or **weitere** as you don't need them to answer the question.

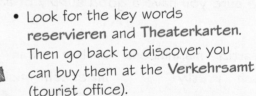

Stadtzentrum hin – to
Stadtzentrum her – from

Where can you book theatre tickets?
At the tourist office.

Now try this

Answer these questions on the text above.

1 What does it say about Rothenburg as a tourist destination?
2 Name **two other** adjectives used to describe Rothenburg.
3 What sort of buildings are there?
4 Where exactly is the tourist office?

Opinions of your town

When you are writing or speaking about where you live, try to discuss the advantages as well as the disadvantages, to include more complex language.

Wie findest du deine Stadt?

Ich wohne ...	I live ...
in einer Stadt	in a town
in einer Großstadt (f)	in a big town/city
in einer Kleinstadt (f)	in a small town
in der Hauptstadt (f)	in the capital city
auf dem Land (n)	in the country
flach / hügelig	flat / hilly
hässlich / schön	ugly / beautiful
historisch	historic
industriell / ländlich	industrial / rural
ruhig / laut	quiet / loud
tot / lebendig	dead / lively
Vorteil / Nachteil (m)	advantage / disadvantage
auf der einen Seite ...	on the one hand ...
auf der anderen Seite ...	on the other hand ...
ehrlich gesagt	to be honest
im Großen und Ganzen	on the whole

Using weil, dass, wo (because, that, where)

Grammar page 95

Don't be worried by conjunctions which send the verb to the end of the sentence. Learn a few key phrases and it will become natural.

Ich wohne nicht gern hier, weil es nichts für Teenager gibt.
I don't like living here because there is nothing for teenagers.

Es ist ein Vorteil, dass ich mit dem Rad in die Schule fahren kann.
It is an advantage that I can cycle to school.

Ich würde lieber in einer Stadt wohnen, wo es mehrere Geschäfte und Clubs gibt.
I would prefer to live in a town where there were more shops and clubs.

Worked example

Beschreib deinen Wohnort.

Ich wohne in einem hässlichen und industriellen Vorort von Genf, wo es nur Gebäude, Fabriken und Büros gibt. Ich würde so gern auf dem Land wohnen, weil die Landschaft dort schön und die Luft frischer ist.

AIMING HIGHER Als Kind lebte ich in einem riesigen Haus mit einem Garten, der einfach wunderbar war, aber letztes Jahr haben sich meine Eltern scheiden lassen und ich bin mit meiner Mutter nach Berlin umgezogen. Jetzt wohnen wir in einer kleinen Wohnung, aber ich wünsche mir jeden Tag, dass ich wieder auf dem Land wohnen würde.

Aiming higher

- Make sure you add CONJUNCTIONS to your work, such as wo (where) and weil (because).
- Use a VARIETY of tenses such as perfect, imperfect, future, present.
- Include GOOD STRUCTURES such as als Kind, haben sich scheiden lassen and ich wünsche mir, dass ...
- Use INTERESTING VOCABULARY such as wunderbar, riesig and winzig.

Giving both opinions (advantages and disadvantages) increases what you can say and gives you the opportunity to use a variety of language.

Now try this

Give three advantages and three disadvantages about the place where you live. Talk for about one minute.

Town description

Giving plenty of facts about your town in your presentation may avoid tricky questions later!

Stadtbeschreibung

Einwohner (mpl)	inhabitants
Gegend (f)	area, region
Gebiet (n) / Umgebung (f)	area
Stadtmitte (f)	town centre
Vorort (m)	suburb
Industrie (f)	industry
Landschaft (f)	landscape
Luftverschmutzung (f)	air pollution
Stadtrand (m)	edge of town
50 Kilometer von ... entfernt.	50 km from ...
in der Nähe von	near to
bekannt	well-known
verschmutzt	polluted

North, South, East, West

im Norden

im Westen

im Osten

im Süden

To say NE, NW, SE, SW:

in Südwestengland – in South-west England

in Nordostschottland – in north-east Scotland

Describing a town

- When saying where a town is, offer plenty of information and include adjectives (malerisch, einmalig) and interesting verbs (zählt, liegt, umgeben).

- Here is an A grade description:
  Knaresborough ist eine malerische Kleinstadt, die ungefähr 15 000 Einwohner zählt. Die Stadt liegt nur 25 Kilometer von Leeds entfernt in Nordengland und ist von einmaliger Landschaft umgeben.

Worked example

Where is Dortmund?

(a) East
(b) North
(c) West ✓
(d) Central
(e) South

– Dortmund ist in Westdeutschland.

- Even if you don't hear the full word **Westdeutschland**, you should pick up the 'v' sound of **West-** so you can rule out east, north and south.

- You will only be able to eliminate central once you have listened to all five recordings.

München – Munich
Köln – Cologne
Wien – Vienna

Now try this

Listen to the rest of the recordings and find out where Hamburg, Dresden, Munich and Kassel are.

You won't hear the word **Zentral-** or **Mitte** to indicate a town in the centre of the country, but you will hear **im Herzen** (in the heart), which tells you that's where this town is.

Holiday destinations

Think about where you like to go on holiday, then think of ways to justify your choice.

Ferienziele

Am liebsten übernachte ich ...	I like staying most of all ...
auf dem Land	in the countryside
an der Küste	on the coast
in den Bergen / im Gebirge	in the mountains
in einer Stadt	in a town
in einem Dorf	in a village
zu Hause	at home
bei Freunden	with friends
weil ...	because ...

man im See schwimmen kann.
you can swim in the lake.

es dort viel wärmer als in England ist.
it is much warmer there than in England.

meine Eltern gern in den Bergen wandern gehen.
my parents like walking in the mountains.

wir dort eine Ferienwohnung haben und wir dort kostenlos wohnen können.
we have a holiday flat there and we can live there free.

Accusative and dative prepositions

Grammar page 89-98

an	on, to
auf	on, to
in	in, into

These use the DATIVE case when there is NO MOVEMENT involved.

Ich wohne im Ausland.   I live abroad.

Das Haus liegt am See.
The house is on the lake.

BUT if there is MOVEMENT towards a place, this signals the ACCUSATIVE case.

Ich fahre ins Ausland.
I am going abroad.

Ich fahre an die Küste.
I am going to the coast.

For other prepositions like this, see page 89.

Am liebsten übernachte ich an der Küste.

Worked example

WRITING

Where do you like to go on holiday?

In den Sommerferien fahren wir immer ins Ausland, weil es dort sonnig und warm ist.

This includes an inverted sentence (**fahren wir**) and a subordinating conjunction (**weil**).

AIMING HIGHER Da ich letztes Jahr in den Ferien zu Hause geblieben bin, fahre ich diesen Sommer an die Küste, damit ich viele Wassersportarten machen kann.

A variety of subordinating conjunctions, such as **nachdem** (after), **bevor** (before) and **damit** (so that) and tenses (perfect, present) are good ways to significantly improve your writing.

Now try this

WRITING

Describe your favourite holiday destination, in about 100 words.

You can also say why you **wouldn't like** to stay there – your sentences do not always have to be full of positives.

Holiday accommodation

Use this page to help you say what type of holiday accommodation you prefer.

Die Ferienunterkunft

Bauernhaus (n)	farmhouse
Bauernhof (m)	farm
Campingplatz (m)	campsite
Ferienwohnung (f)	holiday flat
Mietwohnung (f)	rented flat
Halbpension (f)	half board
Hotel (n)	hotel
im Voraus	in advance
inbegriffen	included
Jugendherberge (f)	youth hostel
mieten	to hire, rent
Pension (f)	bed and breakfast place
übernachten	to stay the night
Übernachtung (f)	overnight stay
Unterkunft (f)	accommodation
Wohnwagen (m)	caravan, mobile home

Gern, lieber, am liebsten

A simple way of showing a preference is to use gern (like), lieber (prefer) and am liebsten (like most of all).

gern ♥
lieber ♥♥
am liebsten ♥♥♥

- Put gern and lieber after the verb:
  Ich schlafe gern im Freien.
  I like sleeping outdoors.
  Ich bleibe lieber im Hotel.
  I prefer staying in a hotel.

- Use am liebsten to start your sentence:
  Am liebsten zelte ich.
  Most of all I like camping.

Ich schlafe lieber im Freien.

Worked example SPEAKING

Wo übernachtest du am liebsten im Urlaub?

AIMING HIGHER Letzten Sommer haben wir in einer Pension übernachtet, aber das war schrecklich, weil wir abends um neun Uhr ins Bett gehen mussten. Diesen Sommer werden wir eine Ferienwohnung mieten und ich freue mich darauf.

Ich finde es ungemütlich, im Zelt zu schlafen, weil es oft so kalt und unbequem ist.

Am liebsten übernachte ich in einem Hotel.

Aiming higher

Include the following in your speaking and writing, to aim for a higher grade.

- ADJECTIVES make your speaking and writing much more ... fascinating, exciting, amusing.
- Think PPF (past, present, future) TENSES before you say anything and then figure out a way to incorporate all three into your answer.
- CONJUNCTIONS give lots of scope for great sentences, so make sure you are confident with weil, wenn and dass, and can also have a go with obwohl, bevor and wo.

Now try this SPEAKING

Answer these questions as fully as you can. Talk for about one minute.

- Wo übernachtest du im Urlaub am liebsten?
- Warum?

Think:
- connectives
- adjectives
- tenses
- conjunctions

Throw each of these in the mix and you are well on the way to a very good answer.

Holiday homes

Use this page to give more detail about where you stay on holiday.

Ferienhäuser

Badezimmer (n)	bathroom
Dusche (f)	shower
Esszimmer (n)	dining room
Garten (m)	garden
Hausordnung (f)	rules of the house
Küche (f)	kitchen
Schlafzimmer (n)	bedroom
Toilette (f)	toilet
Treppe (f)	staircase
Untergeschoss (n)	basement
Wohnzimmer (n)	sitting room
Bettwäsche (f)	bedlinen
frei / besetzt	free / booked
Heizung (f)	heating
möbliert	furnished
Schlüssel (m)	key
Vorhang (m)	curtain
im Erdgeschoss	on the ground floor
im zweiten Stock	on the second floor
auf der ersten Etage	on the first floor

Der, die, das, die (the)

Grammar page 87

Three genders and a plural make up the German words for 'the'.

der – masculine	
die – feminine	die – all plurals
das – neuter	

If two or more German words are combined (as they often are), it is the LAST word which gives the whole word its gender.

Kleider (npl) + Schrank (m) ➡
DER Kleiderschrank (m) – cupboard

Bett (n) + Tuch (n) ➡
DAS Betttuch (n) – sheet

Bad (n) + Wanne (f) ➡
DIE Badewanne (f) – bathtub

Letztes Jahr haben wir in einem Ferienhaus gewohnt.

Worked example

🎧 27   target D

Listen. What did this family book online?
Holiday flat

– Letzten Sommer haben wir eine Ferienwohnung an der Ostseeküste gemietet.

Read the question word very carefully – what? You are listening for a **type** of accommodation, not a date (when?) or a location (where?).

Unknown words

- The BAD news is that, even if you learnt every single word in this book, you are still likely to meet unfamiliar words in assessments. The GOOD news is, you might not need to know them to answer the questions, so don't be put off by words you don't recognise.

- For example, in the Worked example you might not know Ostseeküste (Baltic Sea), but you can still answer the question correctly.

Now try this

🎧 28   target D

Listen again and answer these questions.

1 What was in the eating area?
2 What was wrong with the snooker table?

Staying in a hotel

Much of the hotel vocabulary on this page is also relevant for staying at a bed and breakfast or a youth hostel.

Im Hotel wohnen

Aufenthaltsraum (m)	games room
Aufzug / Fahrstuhl (m)	lift
Fitnessraum (m)	gym
Klimaanlage (f)	air conditioning
Satellitenfernsehen (n)	satellite TV
Schwimmbad (n)	pool
Fenster (n)	window
Gast (m)	guest
Gepäck (n)	luggage
Koffer (m)	suitcase
Reservierung (f)	reservation
auspacken	to unpack
familienfreundlich	family friendly
funktionieren	to work
mit Blick auf	with a view of

Relative pronouns

Grammar page 96

Use a relative pronoun to describe somebody WHO is doing something.

Relative pronouns send the verb to the end of the clause, just like weil (because) and wenn (if).

Der Mann, der (m) im Hotel übernachtet, sitzt oft auf dem Balkon.
The man, who is staying in the hotel, often sits on the balcony.

Die Familie, die (f) hier war, war sehr unfreundlich.
The family, who was here, was very unfriendly.

Das Kind, das (n) im Schwimmbad ist, kann sehr gut schwimmen.
The child, who is in the pool, can swim very well.

Worked example

  READING *target D*

Read the text.

> Die Reise im Frühling hat viel Spaß gemacht. Das war das beste Ostern meines Lebens! Wir haben in einem Drei-Sterne-Hotel gewohnt, das einen Fitnessraum, ein Schwimmbad und eine Sauna hatte. Glücklicherweise gab es in jedem Zimmer Satellitenfernsehen, damit mein Bruder sich nie langweilen konnte. Am Ende des Aufenthalts haben wir alle versprochen, die Zimmer nächstes Jahr wieder zu reservieren. Es war ein einmaliger Urlaub!

Put a cross in the correct box below.

The trip was in …

(a) spring. ☒   **(b)** summer. ☐   **(c)** autumn. ☐

EXAM ALERT!

Students found it tricky to identify the correct information from the text here and were misled by the first recognisable word in a sentence. You must read the whole sentence carefully in the text and not jump to the wrong conclusions.

Students have struggled with exam questions similar to this – **be prepared!**   ResultsPlus

Planning a holiday report for your writing assessment? Use some of these ideas to help you.

Now try this

  READING *target D*

Read the rest of the text and put a cross in the correct box.

1 The hotel had a …
   (a) spa. ☐
   (b) garden. ☐
   (c) gym. ☐

2 The writer's brother was …
   (a) bored. ☐
   (b) entertained. ☐
   (c) ill. ☐

3 Next year they will …
   (a) return to the same hotel. ☐
   (b) go camping. ☐
   (c) stay at home. ☐

Staying at a campsite

Most of the vocabulary for this topic will also be useful for other types of holiday accommodation.

Auf dem Campingplatz

im Freien	in the open air
im Wohnwagen (m)	in a caravan
im Zelt (n)	in a tent
Schlafsack (m)	sleeping bag
Feld (n)	field
Grill (m)	barbecue
Hügel (m) / hügelig	hill / hilly
Insel (f)	island
Meer (n) / See (f)	sea
Natur (f)	nature
See (m)	lake
Wald (m)	wood / forest
Wanderweg (m)	walk / trail
buchen	to book
reservieren	to reserve
wandern	to walk / hike
zelten	to camp

Giving location details

Here are some ways of letting someone know where you live or are staying.

am	at / on
dort	there
entfernt	away from
hier	here
in der Nähe von	near to
neben	near

Der Campingplatz … The campsite …	liegt in der Nähe von Lindau. is near to Lindau.
	ist etwa 30 Gehminuten vom Stadtzentrum entfernt. is about 30 minutes on foot from the town centre.
	liegt am Bodensee. is on Lake Constance.
	befindet sich am Waldrand. is situated on the edge of the wood.

Worked example

Listen and put a cross by **one** facility that is mentioned for this campsite.

(a) Tent and caravan pitches
(b) Baths
(c) Modern wash facilities
(d) Power outlets
(e) Drinking fountains
(f) Boat hire ✗
(g) Football boot hire

– Herzlich willkommen auf dem Campingplatz Maria am Bodensee. Neu ist dieses Jahr unser Bootsverleih (Kajak und Kanu) am Ort. Bitte melden Sie sich bei unserem Bootsmanager.

- Identify language which is not needed for the question. Here, the first couple of words are 'padding' and can be ignored. They don't offer any information about a facility.

- Use all the clues provided. Don't be worried by **Bootsverleih** when you hear it mentioned. The cognates **Boot**, **Kajak** and **Kanu** along with the context of a campsite on Lake Constance should lead you to its meaning: boat hire.

Bodensee – Lake Constance

Now try this

Listen to the rest of the recording and identify the **three** other facilities mentioned.

Only cross **four** things in total, as that is all you have been asked for.

Holiday preferences

What sort of holiday do you like – sporty, lazy, chilled? As well as saying what you DO enjoy doing, make sure you can say what you DON'T enjoy.

Thinking positively

Ich mache gern Urlaub in (Amerika).
I like going on holiday to (America).

Ich ziehe (Aktivurlaube) vor.
I prefer (active holidays).

Am liebsten (bleibe ich im Hotel).
Most of all (I like staying in a hotel).

Mein Lieblingsurlaub wäre (eine Woche in der Türkei).
My favourite holiday would be (a week in Turkey).

Urlaub mit Freunden finde ich …	I find holidays with friends …
ausgezeichnet	excellent
entspannend	relaxing
locker	relaxed / chilled
super / prima	super

Ich fahre nicht gern (ins Ausland).
I don't like going (abroad).

(Sporturlaube) kann ich nicht ausstehen.
I can't stand (sports holidays).

Ich würde nie Skiurlaub machen.
I would never go on a skiing holiday.

(Eine Woche in der Sonne) interessiert mich nicht.
(A week in the sun) doesn't interest me.

Es gefällt mir gar nicht, (die Sehenswürdigkeiten zu besuchen).
I don't like (visiting the sights) at all.

Familienurlaub finde ich … I find family holidays …	ermüdend.	tiring.
	schlecht.	bad.
	schrecklich.	terrible.
	stressig.	stressful.

Urlaub mit Freunden finde ich prima.

Skiurlaube interessieren mich nicht.

Worked example

Although this is an accurate answer, it does little to show higher skills.

Describe your ideal holiday.

Ich fahre in den Ferien sehr gern an das Meer. Ich bin Wassersportfan. Ich windsurfe gern. Ich liebe Segeln.

AIMING HIGHER In den Sommerferien fahre ich sehr gern ans Meer, da ich ein ziemlich großer Wassersportfan bin. Ich windsurfe äußerst gern, aber am liebsten segele ich. Segeln ist meine Leidenschaft.

To improve your writing:
- Add more detail, here by just adding **Sommer** + **ferien**.
- Add an adjective.
- Include a **da** (because, since) (or **weil**) clause – with verb to the end!
- Add **am liebsten** to express preference and combine your sentences with the connective **aber**.

Now try this

Use the techniques listed above to improve your writing.

Write 100 words about your ideal holiday.

Holiday activities

For more things you might do on holiday, look at the leisure activities on pages 10 and 11.

Urlaubsaktivitäten

Man kann ...

bergsteigen gehen

segeln

eislaufen gehen

Ski fahren

faulenzen

spazieren gehen

Rad fahren

Tennis spielen

schwimmen gehen

Saying what you can do

The verbs on the left are in the infinitive form – you need to use this form after the expression Man kann ... (you can ...).

Man kann ...	ins Freibad gehen.
You can ...	go to the pool.
	sich sonnen. sunbathe.

If you start your sentence with a time or place expression, kann and man swap places.

In den Alpen kann man ...
In the Alps you can ...

In den Ferien kann man reiten.
In the holidays you can go horse riding.

Worked example READING target E

Read this text about a holiday.

Verbringen Sie bei uns mitten im Schwarzwald entspannende Tage!

Hier kann man
- viele Sportarten ausprobieren (Bogenschießen, Klettern, Wasserski).
- herrliche Spaziergänge im Wald machen.
- Tagesausflüge nach Freiburg machen.
- den Freizeitpark mit Wildwasserrutschen besuchen.

Put a cross by **one** activity mentioned.

day trips	☐	skiing	☐	theme park	☐
cycling	☐	walking	☐	diving	☒	☐
climbing	☐	tennis	☐	archery	☐

Dealing with unknown words

- Break words down to understand them.
  - schwarz (black) + Wald (wood) = Black Forest
  - frei (free) + Zeit (time) + Park (park) = fun/theme park
  - Bogen (bow) + schießen (shoot) = archery
  - wild (wild) + Wasser (water) + rutschen (slide) = white water slides
- Use any other clues in the text. For example, Bogenschießen is listed as a sport and Wildwasserrutschen can be found in a theme park.

Now try this READING target E

Complete the activity above by putting a cross by the **four** other activities mentioned.

Booking accommodation

If you're booking accommodation, you can't avoid dates, so make sure you are confident with recognising and expressing them. See page 1 for the months of the year.

Unterkunft reservieren

Einzelzimmer (n)	single room
Doppelzimmer (n)	double room
Mehrbettzimmer (n)	shared room
Zweibettzimmer (n)	twin room
Rezeption (f)	reception
Halbpension (f)	half-board
Vollpension (f)	full board
Aussicht (f)	view
Balkon (m)	balcony
mit Seeblick	with a sea / lake view
buchen	to book
inbegriffen / inklusive	included
preiswert / günstig	value for money
reservieren	to reserve

Making a request

You can just ask for things by adding bitte to the end: Ein Einzelzimmer, bitte. But it's more polite, and so much better, to use a conditional:

Ich möchte bitte ein Einzelzimmer reservieren. I would like to reserve a single room.

Ich hätte gern ein Zimmer mit Balkon. I would like a room with a balcony.

Wir möchten bitte ein Doppelzimmer reservieren. We would like to reserve a double room.

Wir hätten gern ein Zimmer mit Halbpension. We would like a room with half-board.

Saying dates

Vom ... bis ... (from ... to ...)

> If you are writing dates, add a full stop after the number: vom 1. bis 14. August.

1st	ersten	3rd	dritten	19th	neunzehnten	22nd	zweiundzwanzigsten
2nd	zweiten	12th	zwölften	20th	zwanzigsten	31st	einunddreißigsten

Worked example

target E

Which booking matches this guest's requirements?

○○○

Ich möchte bitte vom dritten bis dreizehnten Juli ein Einzelzimmer reservieren. Ich hätte, wenn möglich, gern ein Zimmer mit Balkon.

(a) Double room, 7 days + sea view ☐
(b) Single room, 10 days + balcony ☒
(c) Single room, 10 days + dinner ☐

Reading puzzle

Doing a reading activity is like detective work – look for the clues and solve the mystery.

- Look for the type of room first – Einzelzimmer, and you can immediately rule out option (a) as that shows a Doppelzimmer.
- Both options (b) and (c) have 10 days, so the date is not going to solve this one for you.
- The remaining clue is either a balcony or a meal. Go back to the text to discover the words mit Balkon (with a balcony) and you've got the answer.

Now try this

Write a booking request for one of the other two sets of details above.

Future holiday plans

Make sure you are confident with a few of the future expressions listed here, so you can include one in your written and speaking assessments.

Zukünftige Ferienpläne

Ich werde	I will ...
In den Ferien wird er ...	In the holidays he will ...
Hoffentlich werden sie ...	Hopefully they will ...
Eines Tages werden wir ...	One day we will ...
nach Australien fahren.	go to Australia.
auf Musiktour gehen.	go on music tour.
meine Cousine besuchen.	visit my cousins.
nächsten Sommer	next summer
nächsten Winter	next winter
nächstes Jahr	next year
in Zukunft	in future
in zwei Jahren	in two years
Ich freue mich (sehr) darauf.	I am (really) looking forward to it.
Wenn ich älter bin, werde ich einen Ferienjob machen.	When I am older, I will get a holiday job.

Future tense
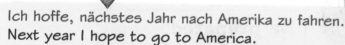
Grammar page 105

The future tense is formed by a part of **werden** (to become) + infinitive.

ich	werde
du	wirst
er / sie / man	wird
wir / Sie / sie	werden

Ich werde nach Ungarn fahren.
I will go to Hungary.

Sie wird Wasserski fahren.
She will go waterskiing.

If you start your sentence with a time expression, werde and ich swap places.

Nächstes Jahr werde ich zu Hause bleiben.
Next year I will stay at home.

You can also use **hoffen + zu** (to hope to) and **möchten** (would like) to indicate future plans.

Ich hoffe, nächstes Jahr nach Amerika zu fahren.
Next year I hope to go to America.

Worked example

WRITING

Write about your future holiday plans.

Ich werde im Sommer nach Spanien fahren.

This is a solid future tense sentence and it's great to have the detail of a time and a place (in the correct order) – but it's not very exciting.

AIMING HIGHER Nächsten Sommer werde ich mit meiner Familie nach Spanien fliegen und wir werden in einer luxuriösen Ferienwohnung an der Küste wohnen. Ich freue mich irrsinnig darauf, weil ich noch nie in Spanien gewesen bin.

This starts with the time phrase **Nächsten Sommer** and inverts the future tense correctly, so **werde** is the next word. The pièce de résistance at the end is the use of the expression **Ich freue mich darauf + weil** followed by the perfect tense.

Now try this

WRITING

Write 100 words about your holiday plans for next year.

Past holidays

Make sure you can use the perfect tense when talking about holidays in the past.

Vergangene Ferien

letzten Sommer	last summer
in den Winterferien	in the winter holiday
letztes Jahr	last year
vor zwei Jahren	two years ago
Ich habe eine Tour gemacht.	I went on a tour.
Er ist nach Rom geflogen.	He flew to Rome.
Wir haben gefaulenzt.	We lazed.

Ich bin Ski gefahren.
I went skiing.

Er hat Bergsteigen gemacht.
He went mountain climbing.

Wir sind schwimmen gegangen.
We went swimming.

Ich habe Camping gemacht.
I went camping.

The perfect tense

 Grammar page 102-3

If you did something in the past, use the perfect tense!

ich habe	gekauft (bought)
du hast	gemacht (did)
er / sie / man hat **+**	besucht (visited)
wir haben	gesehen (saw)
ich bin	gegangen (gone)
du bist	geflogen (flew)
er / sie / man ist **+**	gefahren (went / drove)
wir sind	

To give your opinion in the past, use Es war + adjective:

Es war...

spektakulär / schön   stinklangweilig / furchtbar

Ich bin nach Berlin gefahren. Es war prima!
I went to Berlin. It was great!

Worked example (LISTENING 31) (target D)

What did this person do last year on holiday?
Put a cross by the correct activity.

(a) Swimming ☐   (c) Camping ☒
(b) Mountain climbing ☐   (d) Skiing ☐
(e) Cycling ☐

– Letzten Sommer bin ich in den Schwarzwald gefahren. Leider habe ich auf dem dreckigsten, lautesten Campingplatz in der Gegend übernachtet. Es war furchtbar.

Be prepared

- READ THE RUBRIC first: this is about 'last year', so you are going to hear past tense sentences.
- LOOK AT THE ENGLISH and think about what German words you might expect to hear.
- Remember – you will hear the extract TWICE, so don't panic if you don't get the answer first time round.

Now try this (LISTENING 32) (target D)

Listen to the rest and match the people to an activity in the listening task above.

Note whether they had a positive or negative holiday experience.

1 ☐ C   2 ☐
3 ☐   4 ☐

Directions

Have a look at this vocabulary and see if you can direct somebody from your house to the shops.

Richtungen

Gehen Sie ...   Go ... (on foot)

Fahren Sie ...   Drive

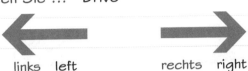

links   left   rechts   right   geradeaus   straight on   um die Ecke / at the corner

über die Brücke / over the bridge   über den Fluss / over the river   zur Ampel / to the traffic lights

an der Kreuzung links / left at the crossroads   zum Kreisverkehr / to the roundabout   auf der linken Seite / on the left

---

Instructions using Sie

Grammar page 99

Use the Sie form (-en) of the verb + Sie:

Überqueren Sie die Straße.
Cross the road.

Gehen Sie an der Ampel rechts.
Go right at the lights.

Instructions using du

Use the du form minus the final -st:

Geh die Einbahnstraße hinunter.
Go down the one-way street.

Learning vocabulary

- Make your own learning cards – German on one side, English on the other; or a picture one side, German on the other.

- Use learning cards to help you learn for your assessments. Write key words on them as well as structures you find tricky.

an der Kreuzung links

Worked example

 LISTENING 33   target C

Listen and choose the correct direction.

(a) Left, then over the crossroads.
(b) Left, then over the bridge. ✗
(c) Right, then round the corner.

– Zum Marktplatz gehen Sie hier gleich links und dann 100 Meter geradeaus. Sie kommen dann zum Fluss, wo es eine Fußgängerbrücke gibt. Gehen Sie hinüber und Sie sehen den Marktplatz auf der rechten Seite.

EXAM ALERT!

In multiple-choice questions, prepare yourself before you listen by trying to say the options to yourself in German. You will be better prepared when you listen!

Students have struggled with exam questions similar to this – **be prepared!**   ResultsPlus

Fluss (river), Fußgängerbrücke (footbridge) and hinüber (over) are the clues to lead you to the answer: (b) over the bridge.

Now try this

 SPEAKING

Give instructions for directions (a) and (c) above.

Travelling

Don't forget the Time – Manner – Place rule when you are saying how you travel somewhere.

Verkehrsmittel

 mit dem Auto / Wagen

 mit der Bahn / mit dem Zug

 mit dem Boot / Schiff

 mit dem Bus

 mit dem Rad (Fahrrad)

 mit dem Flugzeug

 mit dem Lastwagen

 mit dem Mofa

 mit dem Motorrad

 mit der Straßenbahn

 zu Fuß

DB = Deutsche Bahn
ICE = Intercity-Express

Time – Manner – Place

> Grammar page 94

A detail of transport counts as Manner, so put it AFTER a Time expression, but BEFORE a Place.

T gestern / heute / letzte Woche / in Zukunft

M mit dem Zug / zu Fuß / mit meiner Familie

P nach London / in die Stadt / über die Brücke

Heute fahre ich mit der U-Bahn in die Stadtmitte.

Ich bin letzte Woche mit der Straßenbahn gefahren.

Worked example

 SPEAKING

Wie kommst du in die Stadt?

Wenn ich samstags mit meinen Freunden in die Stadt fahre, nehmen wir immer die U-Bahn.

Ich finde, dass sie/die U-Bahn zuverlässig und praktisch ist.

AIMING HIGHER Ich muss nie länger als fünf Minuten warten und jeder Zug kommt pünktlich an.

> Great use of singular ich fahre and plural wir nehmen structures.

> Giving an opinion with Ich denke / finde, dass ... raises the level of your speaking.

> This student has added a modal verb and used a comparative adjective, which raises the level more.

Now try this

 SPEAKING

Answer the questions with as much detail as possible. Talk for about one minute.
- Wie fährst du in die Stadt? Warum?
- Wie fährst du in Urlaub? Warum?

Transport

You may well meet transport vocabulary in a reading text. Watch out for words like nie (never), jeder (every) and trotz (despite). They can be crucial for meaning.

Verkehrsmittel

Autobahn (f)	motorway
Benzin (n)	petrol
bleifrei	lead free
Fahrpreis (m)	fare
Fahrradweg (m)	cycle path
Fahrt (f)	journey
Motor (m)	engine
öffentliche Verkehrsmittel (npl)	public transport
Passagier (m)	passenger
Stau (m)	traffic jam
Tankstelle (f)	petrol station
Umleitung (f)	diversion
Verkehr (m)	traffic
Verschmutzung (f)	pollution
Verspätung haben	to be delayed

Opinions

Use Ich glaube, dass (I believe that) or Ich finde, dass (I think that) as handy ways to add an opinion. Dass sends the verb to the end of the clause.

Fahrradwege sind ausgezeichnet.
Cycle paths are excellent. ➡

Ich finde, dass Fahrradwege ausgezeichnet sind.
I think that cycle paths are great.

Here are some other adjectives you could use when talking about transport:

bequem	comfortable
praktisch	practical
pünktlich	punctual
schädlich	harmful
umweltfreundlich	environmentally friendly

Worked example

Read the text.

> Meiner Meinung nach sollte jeder versuchen, öfter mit der Bahn zu fahren, weil die steigenden Benzinpreise und die Umweltprobleme das Autofahren immer unakzeptabler machen.

Name **two** reasons why Barbara thinks people should travel by train more.

1 Rising petrol prices.
2 Environmental problems.

EXAM ALERT!

When you are asked a question in English you have to **answer** in English. You will not score if you answer in German. Also, if the question asks for **two** reasons, make sure you don't write one or three. If you write three, the third one will be ignored.

> Students have struggled with exam questions similar to this – **be prepared!**   Results**Plus**

The first part of the sentence tells you that Barbara thinks people should travel by train more – so it is the next part which will provide your answer.

Now try this

Read the text and answer the questions **in English**.

> Jake aus Nottingham:
> Ich bin Austauschschüler in Berlin. Ich finde, es ist erstaunlich, wie viel besser die öffentlichen Verkehrsmittel hier in Berlin sind als bei mir zu Hause in England. Wenn man bei uns mehr Geld in Züge investieren würde, könnten wir vielleicht auch stolz auf unser Verkehrsnetz sein!

erstaunlich – incredible
stolz auf – proud of

1 What does Jake think of the public transport in Berlin?
2 What would make it better in England?

At the café

Lots of these food words look very similar to English, so you should recognise them in a reading or listening passage.

Im Café

Ich habe ... bestellt.	I ordered ...
Fruchtsaft (m)	fruit juice
Limonade (f)	lemonade
Mineralwasser (n)	mineral water
Ich hätte gern einmal ...	I would like a (portion of) ...
Fisch (m)	fish
Hähnchen (n)	chicken
Hamburger (m)	hamburger
Nudeln (fpl)	pasta
Omelett (n)	omelette
Pommes (frites) (pl)	chips
Schaschlik (m)	kebab
Eis (n)	ice cream
Frucht (f) / Obst (n)	fruit

Saying 'how many'

- Use number + mal (all one word, lower case) when ordering food portions:

  Ich möchte bitte einmal Pommes frites mit Ketchup.
  I'd like one portion of chips with ketchup, please.

- Use the same construction when talking about how often you do something:

  Letztes Jahr bin ich dreimal pro Woche ins Café gegangen.
  Last year I went to the café three times a week.

Guten Appetit!

There are many sausage varieties in Germany, so make sure you are familiar with these:

Bockwurst – bockwurst
Bratwurst – fried sausage
Currywurst – curried sausage

mit – with
ohne – without
Ketchup – ketchup
Mayonnaise – mayonnaise
Senf – mustard

Bratwurst mit Senf

Worked example

LISTENING 34 target F

What does Mohammed order at the snack bar?

(a) ☐   (d)  ☐
(b) ☐   (e) ☒
(c) ☐   (f) ☐

– Was möchtest du, Mohammed?
– Ein Eis, bitte.

EXAM ALERT!

The topic of food is very familiar and this sort of task offers a good opportunity for you to do well – but some students made mistakes because they did not know this basic vocabulary.

This was a real exam question that a lot of students struggled with – **be prepared!**

 ResultsPlus

Now try this

LISTENING 35 target F

Note: one of the pictures is not needed.

Now listen and note what Martin, Christian, Didi and Markus order.

Eating in a café

Think of ways of including this food vocabulary into your assessments – it could be a description of a special occasion or a disastrous meal out last week.

Im Café essen

Bier (n)	beer
Braten (m)	roast
Fleisch (n)	meat
Frikadelle (f)	meatball
Gemüse (n)	vegetable
Kotelett (n)	chop
Salz und Pfeffer	salt and pepper
Schnitzel (n)	escalope
Schweinekotelett (n)	pork chop
Soße (f)	sauce / gravy
Suppe (f)	soup
Wein (m)	wine
Bedienung (f)	service
Erfrischungen (fpl)	refreshments
Imbissstube (f)	snack bar
Schnellimbiss (m)	snack bar
Selbstbedienung (f)	self-service
Stehcafé (n)	café where you stand up

Using wenn

Grammar page 106

Try to slip in a complex sentence like this to significantly improve your speaking/writing work.

Wenn ich Hunger hätte, würde ich Frikadelle mit Pommes bestellen.
If I were hungry, I would order meatballs and chips.

Wenn ich Vegetarier wäre, würde ich meistens italienisch essen.
If I were a vegetarian, I would eat mostly Italian food.

Salat —
Pommes —
Steak —

Worked example

 LISTENING 36   target E

What does Melissa order?
A Pork and a drink ☐
B Pork and chips ☒
C Lamb chop and chips ☐

- Was möchten Sie?
- Ich möchte Schweinekotelett bitte.
- Sonst noch etwas?
- Ja, eine Portion Pommes bitte.
- Etwas zu trinken?
- Nein danke.

Listening strategies

- People sometimes change their minds, so don't assume they are ordering EVERY ITEM of food you hear mentioned.

- Make sure you listen carefully for what the person ACTUALLY orders. It might not be what they originally wanted, or they might be offered something else which they don't want.

- Listen for phrases such as Es tut mir leid (I'm sorry) which might tell you that something is NOT available.

Now try this

 LISTENING 37   target E

Listen to the rest of the recording. What do Oliver and Susanne order? Put a cross in the correct box.

1 Oliver:
  A Beer and soup ☐
  B Tea and soup ☐
  C Tea and bread ☐

2 Susanne:
  A Apple juice and meatballs ☐
  B White wine and sausage ☐
  C White wine and meatballs ☐

At a coffee house

Make sure you know how to ask for a cup of tea or coffee – or a piece of cake.

In der Kaffeestube

Flasche (f)	bottle
Früchtetee (m)	fruit tea
Glas (n)	glass
Kaffee (m)	coffee
Kakao (m)	cocoa
Kännchen (n)	pot
Kräutertee (m)	herbal tea
Mineralwasser (n)	mineral water
Tasse (f)	cup
Tee (m)	tea
ohne / mit Milch (f)	without / with milk
Sahne (f)	cream
Zitrone (f)	lemon
Zucker (m)	sugar
Brötchen (n)	roll
hausgemacht	home-made
Imbiss (m)	snack
Kuchen (m)	cake
Portion (f)	portion
Stück (n)	piece
Torte (f)	gateau

Indefinite article (a, an)

Grammar page 88

Masculine nouns

- nominative – ein
  Ein Kaffee kostet 3 Euro.
  A coffee costs 3 euros.
- accusative – einen
  Ich hätte gern einen Kaffee.
  I'd like a coffee.

Feminine nouns

- nominative and accusative – eine
  Eine Torte kostet 13,50 Euro.
  A cake costs 13.50 euros.
  Ich hätte gern eine Torte.
  I'd like a cake.

Neuter nouns

- nominative and accusative – ein
  Ein Käsebrot kostet 4 Euro.
  A cheese sandwich costs 4 euros.
  Ich hätte gern ein Käsebrötchen.
  I'd like a cheese roll.

eine Tasse Tee – a cup of tea
ein Stück Torte – a piece of gateau

Worked example

 target **D**

Answer the question in English.

What type of drink is this website advertising?

Coffee.

Bei uns erleben Sie ein reiches Aroma und einen cremigen Kaffeegeschmack. Sie können eine milde Tasse oder einen starken Espresso genießen. Egal, ob Sie Ihre tägliche Tasse mit oder ohne Milch bevorzugen, bei uns finden Sie bestimmt etwas!

EXAM ALERT!

A small minority of students continue to answer the English questions in German and thus sadly miss out on scoring any marks.

This was a real exam question that a lot of students struggled with – **be prepared!**

ResultsPlus

Do not write down **Kaffee** – the answer has to be in English: coffee.

Now try this

 target **D**

According to the website advert:

1 What is an espresso's quality?
2 How often should people drink a cup?
3 What might or might not people add to their cup?

At a restaurant

When talking about a visit to a restaurant, always try to include adjectives in your work and impress with correct endings.

Im Restaurant

Auswahl (f)	selection / choice
Speisekarte (f)	menu
Speisesaal (m)	dining room
Spezialität (f)	speciality
Tagesgericht (n)	dish of the day
Menü (n)	set meal
Getränk (n)	drink
Vorspeise (f)	starter
Hauptgericht (n)	main course
Nachspeise (f)	dessert
Gabel (f)	fork
Geschirr (n)	crockery
Löffel (m)	spoon
Messer (n)	knife
Serviette (f)	serviette, napkin
Teller (m)	plate
gebraten	roast
gekocht	cooked
gemischt	mixed

Adjective endings (der, die, das)

 Grammar page 91

Masculine nouns

nom	acc	dat	
der gute	den guten	dem guten	Mann Hund Tisch

Feminine nouns

nom / acc	dat	
die gute	der guten	Frau Katze Oma

Neuter nouns

nom / acc	dat	
das gute	dem guten	Kind Getränk Buch

Plural nouns

nom / acc	dat	
die guten	den guten	Freunde Servietten

 Worked example LISTENING 38 target A

Stefan is describing a recent visit to a restaurant. Answer the questions in English.

Where is the restaurant?

Opposite the cathedral.

How did Stefan find out about it?

From his German friend's blog.

- Welches Restaurant hast du besucht?
- Das neue, dem Dom gegenüber. Mein deutscher Freund hatte es auf seinem Blog beschrieben.

EXAM ALERT!

Some students failed to cope with the more open-ended format of this question and, even if they understood the listening material, did not answer with enough precision to be awarded the marks. For example, **gegenüber** was known by only a few students; most wrote 'near the cathedral', which was not accurate enough.

This was a real exam question that a lot of students struggled with – be prepared! ResultsPlus

Cognates are easy to spot when you see them, but they can sound slightly different – here **Blog** sounds more like 'block', so ask yourself block – blog – which is more likely?

 Now try this LISTENING 39   target A

Now listen to the next part of the recording and answer these questions.

1 What particularly attracted Stefan to this restaurant?
2 Why does he mention €15?

Food opinions

If you are giving an opinion on food (or anything else), always justify it: 'I would recommend the restaurant BECAUSE the staff are so friendly.'

Meinungen über das Essen

mein Lieblingsessen	my favourite food
lecker/schmackhaft	tasty
(un)gesund	(un)healthy
ekelhaft/eklig	disgusting
salzig	salty

Es hat mir (nicht) geschmeckt. I did(n't) like it.

Ich würde das Restaurant (nicht) empfehlen.
I would (not) recommend the restaurant.

Es gab eine große / kleine Auswahl an Gerichten.
There was a big / small selection of dishes.

Meiner Meinung nach war es teuer / billig.
In my opinion it was expensive / cheap.

Ich fand die Vorspeise zu scharf.
I found the starter too spicy.

Das Hähnchen hat besonders gut geschmeckt.
The chicken was particularly tasty.

Ich kann Fastfood nicht ausstehen/leiden.
I can't stand fast food.

Time expressions

Add time expressions wherever you can.

ab und zu	now and again
dann und wann	now and then
immer	always
manchmal	sometimes
nie	never
oft	often
selten	seldom

Remember to make sure the verb always comes in second place:
Ich esse manchmal im Café.
I sometimes eat at the café.
BUT
Manchmal esse ich im Café.

 **Worked example** (LISTENING 40) (target A)

The interview from page 49 continues. Answer the question in English.

Why was Stefan's sister disappointed?
The soup was too salty.

- Hat das Essen geschmeckt?
- Mir ja, aber meine Schwester fand die Suppe sehr salzig.

 EXAM ALERT!

Many students were not precise enough in their answers. They did not realise that it was specifically the soup that was salty and so did not answer correctly. You must avoid giving vague answers.

This was a real exam question that a lot of students struggled with – **be prepared!** ResultsPlus

If you don't understand **unhöflich** (rude), it is still worth hazarding a guess after the second hearing rather than leaving a blank. The speaker's **tone of voice** indicates it is something negative, so guess a negative characteristic a waiter might have.

 Now try this (LISTENING 41) (target A)

Answer the final questions on the listening section.

1 How did Stefan describe the waiter?

2 Why would Stefan recommend the restaurant to friends. Give **two** reasons.

Alarm bells should be ringing here – you must write down **two** reasons to answer the question completely.

Restaurant problems

Complaining in a restaurant is a great topic for showing you can use the imperfect tense.

Probleme im Restaurant

Besteck (n)	cutlery
Herr Ober!	Waiter!
Kellner (m) / Kellnerin (f)	waiter/waitress
Kunde (m) / Kundin (f)	customer
Kreditkarte (f)	credit card
Pizzeria (f)	pizzeria
Rechnung (f)	bill
Tischtuch (n)	tablecloth
Trinkgeld (n)	tip
Wahl / Auswahl (f)	choice / selection
dunkel / hell	dark / bright
schmutzig	dirty
schockierend	shocking
servieren / bedienen	to wait (serve at table)
teuer / preisgünstig	expensive / good value
unfreundlich	unfriendly
unhöflich	rude

Imperfect tense

Es ist teuer.	It is expensive. ➡
Es war teuer.	It was expensive.
Ich habe Hunger.	I'm hungry. ➡
Ich hatte Hunger.	I was hungry.
Es gibt kein Besteck.	There's no cutlery. ➡
Es gab kein Besteck.	There wasn't any cutlery.

Note the PLURAL forms:

Die Tischtücher waren schmutzig.
The tablecloths were dirty.

Meine Freunde hatten Hunger.
My friends were hungry.

Es gab viele Gläser.   There were a lot of glasses.

Worked example

WRITING

Write about a bad experience in a restaurant.

AIMING HIGHER Früher bin ich immer gern essen gegangen, aber seitdem ich in der Pizzeria Georgio war, denke ich jetzt, dass ich nie wieder in ein Restaurant gehen werde. Es war ein schockierendes Erlebnis, das gar keinen Spaß gemacht hat. Erstens war das Restaurant sehr schmutzig und dunkel. Zweitens gab es keine Pizza! Der Holzofen war kaputt und der Chefkoch konnte nur Salate und Nachspeisen zubereiten. Und drittens war die Rechnung am Ende des Abends ein Skandal, da sie unglaublich teuer war.

Aiming higher

- Use different TENSES but check they are the correct ones and that they make sense.
- Use KEY WORDS to help identify the tense:
  - früher (earlier) and seitdem (since) + a past tense.
  - jetzt (now) for the present.
  - nie wieder (never again) indicates the future.
- Try to include a RELATIVE CLAUSE somewhere in your writing assessments.
- Don't overuse a conjunction. Replace weil (because) with da (since) or denn (for).

Now try this

WRITING

Write 100 words about a restaurant experience. See how many tenses you can include.

Follow the structure of the example above and adapt it for your own experience – real or imaginary.

Shops

Although the list of shops might look long, you'll be surprised at how many shops you already know because you recognise part of the word.

Die Geschäfte

Apotheke (f)	chemist's (with prescriptions)
Drogerie (f)	chemist's (no prescriptions)
Bäckerei (f)	bakery
Blumenladen (m)	florist
Buchhandlung (f)	bookshop
Fleischerei / Metzgerei (f)	butcher
Friseur (m)	hairdresser
Juweliergeschäft (n)	jeweller's
Kaufhaus (n)	department store
Kleidungsgeschäft (n)	clothes shop
Konditorei (f)	cake shop
Lebensmittelgeschäft (n)	grocer's
Möbelgeschäft (n)	furniture shop
Obst- und Gemüseladen (m)	greengrocer's
Schreibwarengeschäft (n)	stationer's
Supermarkt (m)	supermarket
Tabakwarengeschäft (n)	tobacconist
Tante-Emma-Laden (m)	corner shop
Zeitungskiosk (m)	newspaper kiosk

Definite article (the)

Grammar page 88

Masculine nouns

nominative – der

Der Kiosk ist teuer.

⬇

accusative – den

Ich finde den Kiosk teuer.

Feminine nouns

nominative and accusative – die

Die Bäckerei ist toll.

Ich finde die Bäckerei toll.

Neuter nouns

nominative and accusative – das

Das Kaufhaus ist preiswert.

Ich finde das Kaufhaus preiswert.

> Look at how many of these shops end in the word for 'shop': das Geschäft or der Laden.

Worked example

target G

What can you buy here?

(a) Flowers.
(b) Fruit. ✓
(c) Newspapers.

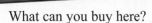
Obstmarkt

- Split the word into **Obst** (fruit) and the cognate **Markt** (market) and see if it reduces your answer options.
- Only (a) flowers and (b) fruit are likely to be bought at a market, so you now have to decide which it is.
- Can you remember the German word for flowers, **Blumen**? If so, you now know that the answer is more than likely to be (b) fruit (**Obst**).

Now try this

target G

Match the names of the shops with the items they sell.

(a) Musikgeschäft
(b) Delikatessengeschäft
(c) Elektrogeschäft
(d) Möbelgeschäft

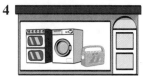

At the market

Learn these items as they could be useful for the healthy eating topic too!

Auf dem Markt

Obst	Fruit	Gemüse	Vegetables
Ananas (f)	pineapple	Blumenkohl (m)	cauliflower
Apfel(˝) (m)	apple	Bohne(-n) (f)	bean
Apfelsine(-n) (f) / Orange(-n) (f)	orange	Champignon(-s)	mushroom
Aprikose(-n) (f)	apricot	Pilz(-e) (m)	mushroom
Banane(-n) (f)	banana	Erbse(-n) (f)	pea
Birne(-n) (f)	pear	Gurke(-n) (f)	cucumber
Erdbeere(-n) (f)	strawberry	Kartoffel(-n) (f)	potato
Himbeere(-n) (f)	raspberry	Knoblauch (m)	garlic
Kirsche(-n) (f)	cherry	Kohl (m)	cabbage
Pfirsich(-e) (m)	peach	Kopfsalat (-e) (m)	lettuce
Pflaume(-n) (f)	plum	Rosenkohl (m)	Brussels sprout
Tomate(-n) (f)	tomato	Spinat (m)	spinach
Traube(-n) (f)	grape	Zwiebel (-n) (f)	onion

Plurals

German nouns all have different plurals. You can look in a dictionary if you are unsure.

An online search for 'Kartoffel plural' gives you the answer instantly:

> Kartoffel (f) (genitive der Kartoffel, plural die Kartoffeln) – potato

The plural word for 'the' is always **die**.

Worked example

READING | **target E**

What is needed from the market? Put a cross in **one** correct box.

(a) ☐

(b) ☐

(c) ☐

(d) ☐

(e) ☐

(f)  ☒

Mama, ich habe die Einkaufsliste zu Hause vergessen. Was muss ich auf dem Markt kaufen?

Meine Güte! Wir brauchen ein Kilo Karotten und eine Gurke für den Gurkensalat.

Ist das alles?

Nein, ich brauche auch dringend ein Kilo Himbeeren für den Nachtisch!

Reading tips

- Go through the text and underline the nouns which are fruit and vegetables – they start with a CAPITAL LETTER.

- Use cognates: Karotten (carrots) and words with a link to an English word. Gurken = cucumbers, from 'gherkin'.

EXAM ALERT!

Remember not to tick or cross more than the required number of boxes – it will count against you.

Students have struggled with exam questions similar to this – be prepared!

ResultsPlus

Now try this

READING | **target E**

Now complete the activity above by putting a cross in **two** more correct boxes.

Food shopping

Here are some more food items and quantities it would be very useful to learn.

Die Lebensmittel einkaufen

Aufschnitt (m)	cold meats
Brot (n)	bread
Joghurt (m)	yoghurt
Honig (m)	honey
Käse (m)	cheese
Kaugummi (m)	chewing gum
Keks (m)	biscuit
Marmelade (f)	jam
Rindfleisch (n)	beef
Saft (m)	juice
Schinken (m)	ham
Schokolade (f)	chocolate
Nudeln (fpl)	pasta
Vollmilch (f)	full fat milk

Quantities

Be careful not to use von (of) with quantities:

 eine Dose + Erbsen =

 a tin of peas

Here are a few more:

ein Dutzend	a dozen
ein Glas	a jar / glass of
eine Packung	a packet of
eine Scheibe	a slice of
eine Tafel	a bar of
eine Tüte	a bag of

Worked example

 LISTENING 42   target C

What did Kerim buy at the corner shop and what did it cost?

Item: a bar of chocolate
Cost: €1.35

– Gestern Nachmittag bin ich zum Tante-Emma-Laden gegangen, weil ich Lust auf Kekse hatte! Im Geschäft habe ich aber eine Tafel Schokolade zum Sonderpreis gesehen, also habe ich sie mir gekauft. Sie hat nur 1,35€ gekostet – sehr günstig, nicht?

The speaker mentions Kekse early on, but carry on listening as he changes his mind and decides to go for the chocolate instead. If you have already jotted down Kekse, cross it out.

Top listening tips

- Make sure you answer BOTH parts of the question to give a complete answer.
- The question asks what the person 'did buy' – be prepared to hear the PAST TENSE.
- DON'T PANIC – you have two chances to get all the information, as you will hear the passage twice.
- JOT DOWN words in English or German when you are doing a listening task – whichever you find easier.
- Make your answers as CONCISE as possible – don't waffle.

Now try this

 LISTENING 43   target C

Listen to the rest of the recording. What did Sophie buy at the supermarket? Note the item and the price.

Shopping

Where there are shops, there's money, so make sure you are familiar with numbers in German (see page 110). Find out how many euros there are to a pound, so you have an idea of prices.

Das Einkaufen

Abteilung (f)	department
Auswahl/Wahl (f)	choice
Bankkarte (f)	bank card
Bargeld (n)	cash
Bedienung (f)	service
Einkaufskorb (m)	shopping basket
Einkaufswagen (m)	shopping trolley
Kleingeld (n)	change, small coins
Konto (n)	bank account
Preis (m)	price
Quittung (f)	receipt
Schaufenster (n)	shop window
billig	cheap
günstig	low priced
herabgesetzt	reduced
preiswert	cheap, value for money
bezahlen / zahlen	to pay
kaufen	to buy
verkaufen	to sell

Money

100 Cents = 1 Euro

 ein 10-Euro-Schein

 ein 2-Euro-Stück

Be careful with -zehn and -zig numbers in prices.

fünfzehn = 15	fünfzig = 50
siebzehn = 17	siebzig = 70

If you are noting down a price you hear, make sure you get the numbers the right way round:

vierunddreißig = 4 + 30 = 34

Worked example

Write about a shopping trip.

Letzte Woche bin ich ins Einkaufszentrum gegangen, aber ich habe nichts gekauft. Meiner Meinung nach war alles zu teuer.

> This uses a past tense **plus** an opinion which makes a solid piece of writing.

AIMING HIGHER

Als ich vor einigen Wochen in der Innenstadt war, habe ich im Schaufenster des Elektrogeschäfts einen stark reduzierten MP3-Spieler gesehen und bin sofort hineingegangen, um ihn zu kaufen. Ich war aber sehr enttäuscht, als der Ladenbesitzer mir erzählte, dass der MP3-Spieler reserviert sei. Seitdem kaufe ich immer im Internet ein, weil dort die Auswahl viel besser ist!

> This is a higher level piece, as it uses:
> - als, da, dass, weil structures
> - an interesting past time phrase
> - an adverb
> - adjectives with correct endings
> - um ... zu ... phrase
> - feelings and opinions
> - a variety of tenses.

> Look at the second writing example above and try to incorporate at least **three** of the elements in your writing.

Now try this

Write 100 words about a recent shopping experience you had.

Shop signs

Make sure you are familiar with this vocabulary from shop signs.

Schilder in den Geschäften

Ausgang / Eingang (m)	exit / entrance
Einkaufszentrum (n)	shopping centre
Ermäßigung (f) / Rabatt (m)	reduction / discount
Lieblingsgeschäft (n)	favourite shop
Notausgang (m)	emergency exit
Winterschlussverkauf (m)	winter (clearance) sale
außer Betrieb	out of order
mit dem Fahrstuhl fahren	to go by lift
an der Kasse zahlen	to pay at the till
im Sonderangebot	on special offer
ausverkauft	sold out
bis zu 70% reduziert	up to 70% reduced
zur Rolltreppe	to the escalator

Dative prepositions

Grammar page 88

aus	from	nach	after
außer	except	seit	since
bei	at	von	from
mit	with	zu	to

(m) der Eingang ➡ zu dem / zum Eingang
(der ➡ dem) – to the entrance

(f) die Kasse ➡ aus der Kasse
(die ➡ der) – from the till

(n) das Geschäft ➡ von dem / vom Geschäft
(das ➡ dem) – from the shop

(pl) die Ausgänge ➡ zu den Ausgängen
(die ➡ den + -n) – to the exits

zu + dem = zum
zu + der = zur
von + dem = vom

Worked example

  target C

Read what Mina says.

Mina: Ich hatte Pech, weil die Blusen alle schon ausverkauft waren.

Which sign did Mina see at the shops?

1 Pay here ☐ 4 Lift out of order ☐
2 Sold out ☒ 5 Open daily from ☐
3 Summer sale starts ☐ nine to six

Ich hatte Pech. – I had bad luck.

Reading tips

• You need to filter the information which is NOT important and focus on that which is.

• Once you have decided on an answer, cross through that text, so you don't waste time considering it again.

Ausverkauft is your key word here: aus = out and verkauft comes from verkaufen = to sell, i.e. answer for (a) – 2. Sold out.

Now try this

  target C

Look back at 1–5 above. Which sign did these people see at the shops?

(a) Finn: Leider war der Fahrstuhl außer Betrieb und ich musste zu Fuß in den vierten Stock gehen! ☐

(b) Emily: Ich freue mich sehr auf morgen, weil in meinem Lieblingsgeschäft dann der Sommerschlussverkauf anfängt. ☐

(c) Niklas: Die Öffnungszeiten sind täglich von neun bis achtzehn Uhr. ☐

(d) Lilli: Als ich zur Kasse kam, merkte ich, dass ich kein Geld dabei hatte! Wie peinlich! ☐

Check your answers at the end to make sure you are happy with your choices.

Clothes and colours

Learn clothes words with their gender, so you can make your adjectives agree.

Die Kleidung und Farben

Anzug (m)	suit
Badeanzug (m)	swimming costume
Badehose (f)	swimming trunks
Bluse (f)	blouse
Gürtel (m)	belt
Hemd (n)	shirt
Hose (f)	trousers
Jacke (f)	jacket
Kleid (n)	dress
Krawatte (f) / Schlips (m)	tie
Mantel (m)	coat
Pullover / Pulli (m)	jumper
Rock (m)	skirt
Schal (m)	scarf
Schuh (m)	shoe
Stiefel (m)	boot
Strumpfhose (f)	tights
Trainingsanzug (m)	tracksuit

Adjective agreements

Grammar page 91

Masculine nouns

nom	acc	dat	
ein roter	einen roten	einem roten	Pulli

Feminine nouns

nom / acc	dat	
eine grüne	einer grünen	Krawatte Mütze

Neuter nouns

nom / acc	dat	
ein blaues	einem blauen	Hemd

Plural nouns

nom / acc	dat	
meine gelben	meinen gelben	Schuhe Jacken

blau gelb lila weiß gestreift

grün rot rosa schwarz kariert

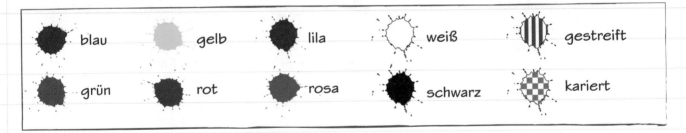

Worked example

LISTENING 44 *target F*

What have these girls bought in town?
Put a cross in the correct box.

1 Olga	☐	☐	☐	☒	☐	☐
2 Fatima	☐	☐	☐	☐	☐	☐
3 Sophie	☐	☐	☐	☐	☐	☐
4 Lisa	☐	☐	☐	☐	☐	☐
5 Anja	☐	☐	☐	☐	☐	☐

```
- Was hast du gekauft, Olga?
- Eine Jacke.
```

EXAM ALERT!

Clothing is a familiar topic and many students got correct answers here. However, a surprising number did not know **Hose** (trousers). Make sure you learn basic vocabulary.

This was a real exam question that a lot of students struggled with – **be prepared!**

  ResultsPlus

Now try this

LISTENING 45 *target F*

Listen to the rest of the recording and complete the activity on the left.

Buying clothes

If you give an opinion on clothes you buy, make sure you justify it with REASONS.

Kleidung kaufen

anprobieren	to try on
bequem	comfortable
Einkäufe (mpl)	purchases
einkaufen gehen	to go shopping
Geschenk (n)	present
Größe (f)	size
Kleidung (f)	clothing
Marke (f)	brand
modisch / schick	fashionable
praktisch	practical
Schlange stehen	to queue
schön	lovely
Umkleidekabine (f)	changing room
Die Jacke ist mir zu groß / klein.	The jacket is too big / small for me.

Accusative prepositions

Grammar page 88

The following prepositions are followed by the accusative case:

durch	through	ohne	without
für	for	um	round
gegen	against		

(m) der Pulli – ohne den Pulli (der ➡ den) without the jumper

(f) die Mutter – für die Mutter (no change) for the mother

(n) das Geschäft – durch das Geschäft (no change) through the shop

(pl) die Einkäufe – für die Einkäufe (no change) for the purchases

---

Worked example

Write about buying clothes.

> Ich liebe Mode. Ich gehe auf dem Flohmarkt einkaufen.

This is correct writing, but look how just a few additions can raise its level …

> Ich liebe Mode und ich gehe oft auf den Flohmarkt, um Klamotten zu kaufen.

This is improved by adding:
- a connective (**und**)
- a time expression (**oft**)
- an **um** ... **zu** ... phrase.

AIMING HIGHER

> Seit meiner Kindheit liebe ich Mode und ich gehe heute immer noch oft auf den Flohmarkt, um mir klassische Klamotten auszusuchen, weil ich sie viel günstiger und interessanter als Markenkleidung finde. Eines Tages werde ich hoffentlich Modedesignerin werden – das ist mein Traum.

To improve your writing still further, also try to add:
- more interesting time phrases (**immer noch heute / eines Tages**)
- a **weil** phrase offering a reason
- a comparison
- a future tense.

Now try this

Write 100 words about your views on buying clothes. Include details of a recent shopping experience.

Use connectives, a time expression and an **um** ... **zu** phrase, as well as at least two tenses.

Returning clothes

This is another topic where you can try to use a range of different tenses.

Kleidung zurücknehmen

beschädigt	damaged
einkaufen	to buy
kaputt	broken
Quittung (f)	receipt
schlechte Qualität	poor quality
schmutzig	dirty
umtauschen	to exchange
zerrissen	torn
Ich möchte das Geld zurück.	I would like the money back.
Es passt mir nicht.	It doesn't fit me.

Es passt / steht mir

Some verbs use a dative pronoun mir, dir, ihm, ihr, uns, ihnen, meaning 'to me / you', etc.

Der Rock passt mir nicht.
The skirt doesn't fit (to) me.

Die Stiefel stehen ihr gut.
The boots suit (to) her well.

Worked example

This man has a problem with a jacket. Complete the sentences by entering the correct letter at the end of each sentence.

Example: The man bought the jacket [f]

1 He is complaining because the jacket ☐
2 He would like to ☐
3 He left the receipt ☐
4 He bought the jacket for ☐

(a) is damaged.
(b) get his money back.
(c) in the car.
(d) at home.
(e) is the wrong size.
(f) last week.
(g) work.
(h) exchange the jacket.
(i) holidays.

– Ich habe letzte Woche diese Jacke bei Ihnen gekauft. Als ich sie heute Morgen anziehen wollte, habe ich darin ein großes Loch gefunden.

EXAM ALERT!

Students generally coped well with this question; however, few realised that **ein großes Loch gefunden** (found a big hole) meant that the jacket was (a) damaged.

Read the question and ALL the choices before you listen. You can start allocating possible answers in your five minutes reading time.

This was a real exam question that a lot of students struggled with – **be prepared!** ResultsPlus

The dialogue is between a male shopper and a female assistant. All the questions relate to 'he', so it is **the man's** sentences which hold the answers.

zurück – back
zurücknehmen – to take back
zurückkommen – to come back
zurückstellen – to put back
zurückfahren – to drive back

Now try this

Listen to both parts of the recording and complete the above activity.

Online shopping

This topic gives you the chance to express lots of opinions, as well as to use the comparative.

Online-Einkaufen ...

hat zahlreiche Vorteile
has countless advantages

spart Zeit
saves time

macht das Leben leichter
makes life easier

bietet eine Riesenauswahl an Produkten
offers a huge range of goods

kann enttäuschend / problematisch sein
can be disappointing / problematic

Comparatives

Use comparatives to say something is faster, quicker, slower, etc.

Online-Einkaufen ist ...	Online shopping is ...
schneller	quicker
einfacher	simpler
billiger	cheaper
besser	better
sicherer	more secure
interessanter	more interesting

Worked example SPEAKING

Ist Online-Einkaufen praktisch?

Wenn man etwas kaufen will, zum Beispiel einen neuen Tisch, sollte man online immer die Bewertungen lesen, bevor man ihn bestellt.

AIMING HIGHER Vor zwei Monaten haben meine Eltern im Internet diesen Tisch gekauft. Mein Vater hat Urlaub genommen und zu Hause auf die Lieferung gewartet. Der Tisch ist aber nicht geliefert worden, weil die Firma in Schwierigkeiten geraten war und keine Lieferungen machen konnte. Seitdem kaufen meine Eltern in der Stadt ein, weil sie kein Vertrauen mehr in Internet-Einkäufe haben.

Aiming higher

- Improve any present tense sentences with interesting CONJUNCTIONS and structures, e.g. zum Beispiel (for example) and Bewertungen (reviews).

- You can talk about a particular online experience and introduce the PAST TENSE, e.g. vor zwei Monaten (two months ago).

- For a top grade, try to include a PASSIVE CONSTRUCTION and an IDIOM, e.g. in Schwierigkeiten geraten (to get into difficulties) and Vertrauen in etwas haben (to trust something).

Now try this SPEAKING

- Choose an unusual or fun picture – fresh subject matter is always welcome.
- Decide if you are going to give a **one** minute presentation on your picture or go straight into a discussion about it.
- Prepare a presentation on this photo.

Make sure you are ready to tackle any unpredictable questions! The more vocabulary and structures relating to your picture you have prepared, the more the discussion will flow.

Shopping opinions

To talk about shopping preferences, you can adapt opinions from other topics, such as food.

Meinungen über das Einkaufen

Einkaufen ist mir egal.
I'm not fussed about shopping.

Einkaufen kann ich nicht ausstehen.
I can't stand shopping.

Geschäfte interessieren mich sehr / nicht.
I find shops very / not at all interesting.

Ich habe nie / immer Lust, einkaufen zu gehen.
I never / always want to go shopping.

Es macht keinen Spaß, einkaufen zu gehen.
Going shopping is no fun

Ich liebe Einkaufen.
I love shopping.

Klamotten sind meine große Leidenschaft.
Clothes are my big passion.

Ich finde Einkaufszentren besser als kleine Geschäfte.
I find shopping centres better than small shops.

Um ... zu...

Grammar page 96

comma + um + nouns/adjs, etc. + zu + verb:

Ich gehe einkaufen, um schicke Kleidung zu kaufen.
I go shopping in order to buy fashionable clothes.

Man muss sich überall umschauen, um hübsche Sachen zu finden.
You have to look around everywhere to find nice things.

Worked example

  target B

Read this text.
Which of the statements is negative? 2

> Letztes Wochenende gab es in Wiesbaden einen verkaufsoffenen Sonntag.
> 1 Viele Käufer, vor allem junge Leute, sind in die Stadt gekommen, um einkaufen zu gehen.
> 2 Die Geschäfte mit trendiger, aber teurer Mode für Jugendliche hatten nur wenige Kunden.
> 3 Shopping gilt heute als Freizeitbeschäftigung Nummer 1.
> 4 Nicht nur die Teenies haben an diesem Sonntag profitiert. Auch viele Käufer über 25 sind in die Stadt gekommen.
> 5 Lukas (15) trägt Zeitungen aus, um Geld für seine Einkäufe zu verdienen: „Einkaufen ist für mich ein Freizeitsport", sagt er fröhlich.

If lots of people came into town to shop, you can assume this a **positive** statement, so not the one you are looking for.

Trendig (trendy) is positive, but don't jump to conclusions. Read on and you discover **teuer** (expensive) and **nur wenige** (just a few) – a **negative** statement after all.

Watch out for negative words which aren't! **Nicht nur** means 'not only', so is in fact a **positive** expression.

The positive adjective **fröhlich** (happily) at the end makes this one clear.

Now try this

  target B

Which **two** of these statements are correct, according to the sentences above?

(a) Young people were the only people to benefit from the Sunday experience. ☐

(b) The top end shops were not popular. ☐

(c) It was mostly old people who went shopping. ☐

(d) Lukas enjoys shopping in his free time. ☐

(e) Shopping has lost popularity recently. ☐

Emergency services

You may find passages about emergency situations in your listening or reading exam – but you could also use some of these phrases in your writing assessment, for example about a holiday disaster.

Notdienst

krank	ill
Krankenhaus (n)	hospital
Krankenwagen (m)	ambulance
Feuerwehr (f)	fire brigade
Feuerwehrmann (m)	fireman
Führerschein (m)	driving licence
Panne (f)	breakdown
Schaden (m)	damage
Verkehrsunfall (m)	traffic accident
Versicherung (f)	insurance
Dieb (m)	thief
Diebstahl (m)	theft
Polizeiwache (f)	police station
Gefängnis (n)	prison
Polizist (m) / Polizistin (f)	police officer

Using als

- Use **als** to mean 'when' in the past tense. Note that it sends the verb to the end, then a comma followed by the next verb.

  Als ich nach Hamburg fuhr, hatte ich eine Panne.

  When I drove to Hamburg, the car broke down.

- But use **wenn** to mean 'when' in the present tense.

  Wenn ich einen Krankenwagen sehe, mache ich mir Sorgen.

  When I see an ambulance, I am worried.

Be careful of these words:
Not – emergency
Notausgang (m) – emergency exit
Notfall (m) – emergency
Notruf (m) – emergency call

Worked example

Write about an experience of an emergency.

Als ich letztes Wochenende unterwegs war, habe ich einen Verkehrsunfall gesehen und ich habe sofort 112 gewählt.

AIMING HIGHER Als ich neulich ins Einkaufszentrum gegangen bin, kam mir ein Junge entgegengelaufen. Er hatte eine Einkaufstasche in der Hand und wurde von einem Polizisten verfolgt. Obwohl ich Angst hatte, war ich sehr mutig und hielt die Tür zu, damit der Polizist den Jungen verhaften konnte.

- This makes good use of **als** to start the sentence, with a time phrase to introduce the past tense.
- The addition of the adverb **sofort** makes the text more interesting.

Aiming higher

- Use separable verbs in the perfect tense – but remember where to put the **ge**.
- Use **obwohl** (although), which works like **als** and sends the verb to the end.
- Include more complex vocabulary: **entgegengelaufen, verfolgt, mutig, hielt zu.**

Now try this

Describe an emergency situation you have experienced in the past in about 100 words.

You can use your imagination here!

Money problems

Be prepared to meet some of this money vocabulary in Higher listening tasks.

Geldprobleme

Bank (f)	bank
Briefmarke (f)	stamp
Fehler (m)	mistake
Kreditkarte (f)	credit card
Problem (n)	problem
Taschengeld (n)	pocket money
Wechselgeld (n)	change
Wechselkurs (m)	exchange rate
Wechselstube (f)	bureau de change
billig / teuer	cheap / expensive
Geld ausgeben	to spend money
wechseln	to change (money)

Ich habe mein Portemonnaie verloren.
I lost my purse.

Ich gebe mein Geld für (Klamotten) aus.
I spend my money on clothes.

Ich habe zu viel Geld ausgegeben.
I spent too much money.

Reflexive verbs (accusative)

Grammar page 98

Ich möchte mich beschweren.
I would like to complain.

Ich freue mich darauf.   I look forward to it.

er/sie + sich: Er freut sich (auf) ...

du + dich: Freust du dich darauf?

wir + uns: Wir freuen uns darauf.

ihr + euch: Freut ihr euch darauf?

Sie + sich: Sie freuen sich darauf.

Ich habe mich entschlossen, das Geld zu wechseln.
I decided to change the money.

Worked example

 LISTENING 48   target C

The Gruber family had problems on a recent trip to London.

Who did what? Complete the sentences.

1 Mrs Gruber [b]
2 Mr Gruber [ ]
3 Martin [ ]
4 Julia [ ]

(a) lost a credit card.
(b) spent too much money.
(c) had to visit the doctor.
(d) did not like English food.

— Ich finde London sehr schön. England ist für uns ziemlich teuer und ich habe viel zu viel Geld ausgegeben.

Listening tips

- The listening passages are not very long, so make sure you really concentrate on EVERY WORD to find the answers.
- The recording will carry on to the next activity after the second listening, so make sure you are not still trying to change answers once the second listening is complete.

EXAM ALERT!

The most difficult part here proved to be **ich habe viel zu viel Geld ausgegeben**, where only half of Foundation students were able to associate this opinion (b) with Mrs Gruber.

This was a real exam question that a lot of students struggled with – be prepared!

ResultsPlus

Now try this

 LISTENING 49   target C

Complete the listening activity above. Listen to the recording twice.

Problems at the station

You may meet vocabulary to do with travel problems in the reading exam, so be prepared!

Probleme am Bahnhof

Ich war / wurde ...	I was / became ...
Wir waren / wurden ...	We were / became ...
empört	indignant
wütend	furious
verlegen	embarrassed
böse/zornig	angry
(un)zufrieden	(dis)satisfied

Der Zug hatte eine Panne.
The train broke down.

Ich habe den Zug verpasst.
I missed the train.

Ich musste 30 Minuten Schlange stehen.
I had to queue for 30 minutes.

Der Zug hatte Verspätung.
The train was late.

Der Fahrkartenautomat war außer Betrieb.
The ticket machine was not working.

Pronouns

Grammar page 93

Pronouns = he, him, their, her, your, our

nominative	accusative	dative
ich	mich	mir
du	dich	dir
er	ihn	ihm
sie	sie	ihr
es	es	ihm
wir	uns	uns
ihr	euch	euch
Sie / sie	Sie / sie	Ihnen / ihnen

Er war wütend.   He was furious.
Er hilft mir.   He helps me.

Das hat sie verärgert.
That annoyed her.

Worked example

READING | target B

Read what these people say about train journeys.

Toby: Ich fahre besonders gern mit der Bahn, obwohl das heutzutage sehr teuer ist.

Sara: Gestern wurde ich am Bahnhof immer wütender, weil ich 30 Minuten Schlange stehen musste.

Elena: Der Fahrkartenautomat war außer Betrieb. So ein Mist!

Lukas: Der Beamte war wirklich unfreundlich und langsam und daher habe ich den Zug verpasst.

Harry: Der Zug hatte Verspätung und ich bin nicht rechtzeitig zur Schule gekommen.

Hanna: Auf der Rückfahrt hatte der Zug eine Panne und wir mussten zwei Stunden im kaputten Zug sitzen.

Who says what? Write down the correct name.
I was late for lessons. Harry.

- You don't have to answer the questions **in order** – if you spot a match, such as (d) expensive and Toby saying **teuer**, put it down and go back to another question.

- Read the English sentences to see if you can find any **parallels** in the German: Schule and lessons might be connected.

- Don't make a careless mistake and **muddle** the names up, i.e. Harry and Hanna.

Now try this

 READING | target B

Complete the activity above by noting down who says each of these.

(a) The ticket machine didn't work.
(b) Our train broke down.
(c) I had to queue for half an hour.
(d) I think trains are expensive.

Lost property

Lots of the revision topics are interlinked – you may well come across lost property vocabulary in a shopping context ... and andersherum (vice versa).

Verlorene Sachen

Brieftasche (f)	wallet
Handtasche (f)	handbag
Kamera (f)	camera
Fotoapparat (m)	camera
Personalausweis (m)	ID card
Portemonnaie (n)	purse
Regenschirm (m)	umbrella
Schlüssel (m)	key
Uhr (f)	watch

Es ist blau und ziemlich groß.
It's blue and quite big.

Sie ist wertvoll.
It's valuable.

Sie ist aus braunem Leder.
It's made of brown leather.

Es ist aus rotem Kunststoff.
It's made of red plastic.

Ich habe sie in der Herrenabteilung verloren.
I lost it in the men's department.

Possessive pronouns

Grammar page 90

These use the same endings as for ein and eine (see page 48).

dein	your	unser	our
sein	your/its	euer	your (pl)
ihr	her/their	ihr	their

Masculine

Ich habe meinen Personalausweis verloren.
I've lost my ID card.

Feminine

Ich habe meine Uhr verloren.
I've lost my watch.

Neuter

Ich habe mein Portemonnaie verloren.
I've lost my purse.

Plural

Ich habe meine Schlüssel verloren.
I've lost my keys.

Worked example

 LISTENING 50   target E

Christian is at the lost property office. Fill in the information in English.

1 Lost Item: wallet
2 When was it lost? ....
3 Colour: ....
4 Where was it lost? ....

– Guten Tag, wie kann ich Ihnen helfen?
– Also, ich habe gerade meine Brieftasche verloren und ich wollte wissen, ob sie jemand gefunden hat.

Listening to dialogues

• 'Official' dialogues, such as at a lost property office or at a police station will use the Sie polite form.

• Don't be worried by hearing a variety of tenses (here the perfect and pluperfect). Just focus on the answers to the questions.

• The ANSWERS to the questions will follow the ORDER of the dialogue.

If you miss the word Brieftasche first time round, you might get a second chance to hear it further along in the dialogue. Leave the space blank for now and come back to it ether later in the dialogue, or on your second listening.

Now try this

  LISTENING 51   target E

Listen to the rest of the recording and answer the remaining questions above.

Complaints

Moan, moan, moan, but how to do it in German? Here are some ideas!

Beschwerden

Es tut mir (furchtbar) leid, aber …	I am (awfully) sorry but …
Ich ärgere mich, weil …	I am angry because …
Ich habe verlangt, mit dem Chef zu sprechen.	
I demanded to speak to the boss.	
Ich habe einen Brief an den Kundendienst geschrieben.	
I wrote a letter to customer services.	
Man hat das Problem schnell gelöst.	
The problem was quickly solved.	
Man hat mir versichert, dass …	
Somebody assured me that …	
hoffen	to hope
lügen	to lie
vermeiden	to avoid
versprechen	to promise
verzeihen	to forgive

Using man

- Use man to mean one / you / somebody / people.
- Man takes the er / sie part of the verb (man hat).

Present tense

Man hilft bei Problemen.
One helps with problems.

Past tense

Man hat einen Brief geschrieben.
Somebody / One wrote a letter.

Future tense

Man wird das verbessern.
One will improve that.

Don't confuse man with der Mann = the man.

Ich habe mich telefonisch darüber beschwert.
I complained about it by phone.

Worked example SPEAKING

Beschreib ein Problem, das du gehabt hast.

AIMING HIGHER Ich gehe wirklich gern mit Freunden ins Café, aber letzten Sommer hatte ich ein schreckliches Erlebnis, als am Tisch nebenan eine Prügelei losging.

- Think about your **opening sentence**. Start off with something to make the listener sit up and want to know more.
- Don't forget you need to ask at least **two** questions. Here, you could ask: Haben Sie je eine Prügelei gesehen?

Using common idioms

Add idioms to your work to help you aim for a higher grade: adapt these ones to whichever tense you are using.

Ich habe / hatte die Nase voll.
I am / was fed up.

X geht mir auf die Nerven.
X gets on my nerves.

Ich verstehe nur Bahnhof.
I don't understand a thing.

Ich habe großes Pech.
I've got really bad luck.

Das fällt mir auf den Wecker.
That really gets up my nose.

Now try this SPEAKING

Explain what happened in this restaurant last summer.
Talk for about one minute.

School subjects

Knowledge of school subject vocabulary is essential for listening and reading exams.

Schulfächer

 Mathe

 Biologie

Chemie

 Physik

 Deutsch

 Englisch

Französisch

Spanisch

Erdkunde

 Geschichte

 Religion

Informatik

 Kunst

Sport

seit + present tense

To talk about how long you have been doing something, use seit + present tense.

Ich lerne seit vier Jahren Deutsch.
I have been learning German for four years.

The noun after seit (since) needs to be in the DATIVE case.

seit vier Monaten ⬅ Dative plurals add -n!
for four months

seit diesem Trimester   for this term

seit letztem Jahr   since last year

seit letzter Woche   since last week

Other useful vocabulary:
Pflichtfach (n) – compulsory subject
Theater – drama
Wahlfach (n) – optional subject
Werken – DT

Worked example

 LISTENING 52   target C

Manni is describing a school day.

Put a cross in the correct box.

When did Manni get to school?

(a) On time. ☐

(b) Late. ☒

(c) Early. ☐

– Am Dienstag bin ich leider zu spät in der Schule angekommen, aber der ganze Tag hat Spaß gemacht.

spät – late
zu spät – too late
die Verspätung – delay

EXAM ALERT!

Almost half of all Higher students did not realise that **zu spät in der Schule angekommen** meant that Manni was late. Knowledge of vocabulary is essential for listening exams.

This was a real exam question that a lot of students struggled with – **be prepared!**

ResultsPlus

Now try this

LISTENING 53   target C

Listen to the whole recording and answer these questions in English.

1 What was Manni's favourite lesson?
2 Why?
3 What did he do during break?

When you have questions in English, make sure your answers really **do** answer the question. English questions normally only need 3–4 words to answer, so **do not** write down everything you hear.

Opinions about school

You need to give lots of opinions – with reasons – about school if you want a higher grade.

Meinungen über die Schule

Meiner Meinung nach ist Chemie einfach.
In my opinion chemistry is easy.

Ich finde, dass Mathe schwierig ist.
I think that maths is difficult.

Es ist gut, dass die Schule so erfolgreich ist.
It is good that the school is so successful.

Die Regeln sind (un)fair / dumm / blöd.
The rules are (un)fair / stupid.

Die Lehrer sind streng / mies.
The teachers are strict / horrible.

Das Schulgelände ist alt / modern.
The school site is old / modern.

Ich habe immer Angst vor den Noten.
I am always afraid of the grades.

Fillers

Use fillers to make you sound more fluent.

bestimmt — certainly
doch — yet, but, however
absolut — absolutely
Fillers
echt — really
sowieso — anyway
klar — clearly
sicher — certainly

Ich finde Deutsch echt super.
I find German really great.

Spanisch ist bestimmt schwierig.
Spanish is certainly difficult.

Mein Lieblingsfach ist auf jeden Fall Werken.
My favourite subject is definitely DT.

In Geschichte habe ich absolut keine Probleme.
I don't have any problems at all with history.

Worked example SPEAKING

Wie findest du die Schule?

Meiner Meinung nach ist Mathe sehr schwierig, besonders wenn man kein fleißiger Schüler ist. Ich finde Sport viel besser, weil wir nie Klassenarbeiten schreiben müssen.

> This student offers a couple of opinions and uses a **modal** with a conjunction, but it is all in the **present** tense.

AIMING HIGHER Es ist absolut fair, dass Rauchen auf dem Schulgelände streng verboten ist, weil Rauchen sowieso schlecht für die Gesundheit ist. Die Schule kann aber stressig sein. Wenn ich schlechte Noten bekomme, werde ich auch ein schlechtes Zeugnis bekommen und dann werden meine Eltern böse sein. In der Grundschule hatte man keine Prüfungen, keinen Stress.

> Look at how this student uses a **variety** of elements and structures to give her opinion of her school:
> - fillers
> - present, future and past tenses
> - modal verb
> - dass, weil and **wenn** clauses.

Now try this SPEAKING

Answer the questions about your school.
- Was ist dein Lieblingsfach? Warum?
- Findest du diese Schule besser als die Grundschule?
- Was magst du besonders an deiner Schule?
- Und was magst du nicht?

School routine

School routine is often chosen as a topic for the speaking or writing assessment, so make sure you can say something a bit unusual to stand out from the others.

Der Schultag

Die erste Stunde beginnt um zehn vor neun.
The first lesson starts at ten to nine.

Wir haben sechs Stunden pro Tag.
We have six lessons each day.

In der Pause gehen wir auf den Schulhof.
At break we go to the playground.

Wir essen zu Mittag in der Kantine.
We eat lunch in the canteen.

Man kann in der Bibliothek Hausaufgaben machen.
You can do homework in the library.

Nach der Schule gibt es ein gutes Angebot an AGs.
After school there is a good selection of clubs.

Sport haben wir immer als Doppelstunde.
We always have a double lesson for PE.

Linking words

> Grammar page 94

These make your sentences longer and DON'T change the word order!

aber   but   oder   or
denn   because   und   and

Man muss viel lernen und ich habe Angst vor den Noten.
You have to learn a lot and I am afraid of the grades.

In der Pause plaudern wir oder wir machen Hausaufgaben
At break we chat or we do homework.

Worked example

READING   target C

Read this text.

Um sechs Uhr wache ich auf, denn der Wecker klingelt und ich muss zur Schule gehen. Ich würde natürlich lieber noch im warmen Bett bleiben, aber das geht leider nicht. Schule ist Pflicht! Ich muss hin! Nach dem Frühstück fahre ich mit der S-Bahn zur Schule. Die Fahrt dauert eine halbe Stunde und unterwegs mache ich Hausaufgaben. Die Schule beginnt um zehn nach acht und ich muss im Klassenzimmer sein, sonst bekomme ich eine Strafarbeit. Als erstes habe ich heute eine Doppelstunde Chemie – mein Lieblingsfach ist das nicht! Ich freue mich aber auf die dritte Stunde, weil wir Sport haben!

What does Beth say about her school routine?
Put a cross in the **four** correct boxes.

(a) School starts at 6 o'clock. ☐
(b) Beth is reluctant to get up. ☒
(c) School is compulsory. ☐
(d) Beth travels by tram to school. ☐
(e) Beth has to do some work on the journey. ☐
(f) Beth has to be in class at ten past eight. ☐
(g) It doesn't matter if she is late. ☐
(h) Beth likes chemistry. ☐

Reading tips

- In this style of activity, the statements will always be in the SAME ORDER as the text.
- Cross through any statements that are WRONG. Here, Beth wakes up at six to go to school, so sentence (a) is clearly wrong.
- If you change your mind about your four answers, make sure you clearly CROSS OUT any answer you don't want.
- Only put crosses in FOUR of the boxes.

Sometimes you have to **infer** meaning. Beth doesn't say explicitly 'I don't like getting up', but the fact that she **would prefer** to stay in the warm bed tells you she is 'reluctant to get up'.

Now try this

READING   target C

Now complete the activity on the left.

German schools

If you talk about schools in your assessment, you could make some comparisons with German schools.

Deutsche Schulen

Direktor (m) / Direktorin (f)	headteacher
Schulleiter (m) / Schulleiterin (f)	headteacher
lernen	to learn
lehren / unterrichten	to teach
Berufsschule (f)	vocational school
Gesamtschule (f)	comprehensive school
Grundschule (f)	primary school
Gymnasium (n)	grammar school
Hauptschule (f)	type of secondary school
Realschule (f)	type of secondary school
Kindergarten (m)	pre-school
Internat (n)	boarding school
Privatschule (f)	private school
Trimester / Semester (n)	term / semester
Zeugnis (n)	report
Klassenkameraden (mpl)	classmates

Using müssen (to have to)

Grammar
page 100

Müssen is a modal verb, so it needs an infinitive:

Man muss Hausaufgaben machen.
You have to do homework.

Man muss ... You have to ...	höflich sein. be polite.
	viel üben, um ein Instrument zu spielen. practise a lot to play an instrument.
	sich ordentlich anziehen. dress smartly.
	sitzen bleiben. repeat a school year.

Man muss pünktlich zur Schule kommen. You have to get to school on time.

Worked example

WRITING

Write about your school experiences.

Ich gehe auf eine Gesamtschule mit etwa tausend Schüler und Schülerinnen. Als ich in die siebte Klasse kam, war ich sehr nervös, weil das Schulgebäude einfach so groß und imposant war.

AIMING HIGHER In der elften Klasse bin ich jetzt viel selbstbewusster und ich fange an, mich richtig auf die Oberstufe zu freuen. Hoffentlich werde ich bei den Prüfungen nicht durchfallen, damit ich nächstes Jahr das Abitur machen kann.

This extract is a good piece of writing, as it includes:
- present and past tense
- opinion + weil + als clause
- an interesting adjective (imposant).

Add some additional features to achieve the best possible type of response:
- inverted sentence
- comparative
- anfangen + zu + infinitive construction
- idiom sich freuen auf
- hoffentlich + future tense.

Now try this

SPEAKING

Write a paragraph of about 100 words to describe your school, using the examples above to help you.

Primary school

Talking about your primary school offers a great opportunity to use the imperfect tense.

Die Grundschule

 Anspitzer (m)   Bleistift (m)   Etui (m)

 Filzstift (m)   Füller (m)   Heft (n)

 Klebstoff (m)   Kuli / Kugelschreiber (m)   Lineal (n)

 Radiergummi (m)  Schere (f) Schreibblock (m)

 Taschenrechner (m) Wörterbuch (n)

Modals – imperfect tense

Grammar page 101

kann – can	→ konnte – could
muss – have to	→ musste – had to
darf – am allowed	→ durfte – was allowed
will – want	→ wollte – wanted
soll – shall	→ sollte – should
mag – like	→ mochte – liked

In der Grundschule … At primary school …	konnte ich kein Französisch sprechen. I couldn't speak French. musste ich mit meiner Mutter zur Schule gehen. I had to go to school with my mum. durfte ich kein Handy benutzen. I wasn't allowed a mobile.

Using an imperfect modal is a good indicator that you are aiming high.

Worked example

READING **target A**

Read the text below.

In der Grundschule habe ich mich immer gut benommen, aber Tim wollte nie machen, was von ihm verlangt wurde. Meine Eltern sagten Tim, dass er mehr wie ich sein sollte. Wenn ich etwas Dummes machte, lachte mein Vater immer, aber mit Tim war er immer böse.

Put a cross next to the correct answer.

When Tim was younger …

A he was not very obedient at school. ☒

B he was a well-behaved pupil. ☐

C he did not go to primary school. ☐

EXAM ALERT!

For this task, good comprehension skills are needed, as well as an ability to draw conclusions from the text. The questions are not phrased in exactly the same way as they appear in the text, so be careful!

Students have struggled with exam questions similar to this – be prepared! ResultsPlus

Now try this

READING **target A**

Read the text again and put a cross by the correct answer.

Their dad reacted to both of them …

A proudly ☐ **B** in the same way ☐ **C** in different ways ☐

Issues at school

Learn a few key phrases to talk about rules and issues at school.

Schulprobleme

Meine Schule hat keinen Chor.
My school hasn't got a choir.

Die Regeln finde ich (un)gerecht.
I find the rules (un)fair.

Im Klassenzimmer darf man nicht essen.
You can't eat in the classroom.

Man darf bei Prüfungen nicht abschreiben.
You are not allowed to copy in exams.

Man muss nachsitzen.
You get detention.

Viele Schüler machen blau / schwänzen.
A lot of students skive.

Viele Schüler leiden unter Schulstress.
Many students suffer from stress at school.

Die Lehrer fehlen oft, weil sie Besprechungen haben.
The teachers are often absent because they have meetings.

Obwohl

Grammar
page 95

Obwohl (although) is a subordinating conjunction which sends the verb to the end of the clause, like weil.

Obwohl es eine kleine Schule ist, gibt es hier viele AGs.
Although it is a small school, there are lots of clubs here.

Er ist zur Schule gegangen, obwohl er schreckliche Kopfschmerzen hatte.
He went to school, although he had a terrible headache.

Wir müssen zu viele Klassenarbeiten schreiben.
We have to do too many tests.

Worked example

Read these signs in school.

(a) Kaugummi im Klassenzimmer verboten!

(b) 34° draußen – heute ist hitzefrei.

(c) Elternabend der 13. Klasse:
1. Mai um 20:00 Uhr.

(d) **Die Ergebnisse der Klassenarbeit sind hier zu finden.**

(e) Bitte nicht eintreten: Besprechung.

(f) Schreibt bei den Abschlussprüfungen nicht ab!

Which sign matches which person?

1 Ralf's school is closed today. | b
2 Teresa can get her results here. | ☐
3 Frau Scheer is in a meeting. | ☐
4 Pupils must not copy in the exam. | ☐
5 Dietmar's parents are due at school this evening. | ☐

Even if you didn't know that **hitzefrei** meant the school was closed because of the heat, you could guess it from the small word **frei** = free (no school).

EXAM ALERT!

Do not read too quickly and make assumptions based on understanding one word. You need to read every word in tasks like this where there is not much text. It might be the smallest of words that holds the answer.

Students have struggled with exam questions similar to this – **be prepared!** ResultsPlus

Now try this

Complete the above activity.

There is only **one** answer for each person, so once you are confident of an answer, cross that sign out and concentrate on the others.

Future education plans

Talking about future plans enables you to say what you WANT to do over the next few years.

Zukunftspläne

Ich möchte / werde ...	I would like to / will ...
das Jahr wiederholen	repeat the year
die Schule verlassen	leave school
eine Prüfung bestehen	pass an exam
einen Studienplatz bekommen	get a college place
einen Ausbildungsplatz bekommen	get a training place
Berufsberater (m)	careers adviser
Berufsschule (f)	vocational college
Kurs (m)	course
Resultat / Ergebnis (n)	result
Mittlere Reife (f)	GCSE equivalent
Abitur (Abi) (n)	A-level equivalent
Abiturient/in (m/f)	student (m/f) with Abitur
Abschlussprüfung (f)	final exam
Qualifikation (f)	qualification
Schulabschluss (m)	school leaving certificate
Student/in (m/f)	student

Using wollen (to want)

Grammar page 100

Wollen is a modal verb, so it needs an infinitive.

Ich will auf die Oberstufe gehen.
I want to go into the sixth form.

> Don't confuse the German will with the English 'will' (future intent). It means 'want to do something'.

Ich will ... I want to ...	weiterstudieren. carry on studying.
	auf die Universität (Uni) gehen. go to uni.
	eine Lehre machen. do an apprenticeship.

Ich will an der Uni Englisch und Geschichte studieren.

Worked example

 SPEAKING   LISTENING 54

Was möchtest du nächstes Jahr machen?

AIMING HIGHER   Gleich nach den Prüfungen will ich ein Wochenende mit meiner Clique an der Küste verbringen. Ich freue mich irrsinnig darauf, obwohl meine Eltern nicht so begeistert darüber sind. Nächstes Trimester werde ich hoffentlich in die Oberstufe kommen, wenn ich die notwendigen Noten bekomme. Ich will Fremdsprachen und Mathe lernen, weil ich eines Tages gern im Ausland arbeiten möchte.

CONTROLLED ASSESSMENT

- Some students fail to talk for **one** minute on their subject so are penalised. Take a deep breath and speak clearly to make sure you last for **one** minute minimum.
- Go for **quality** not quantity and allow plenty of time for interaction to show off your understanding and responding skills.
- Students who repeat their presentation language in the following discussion do not impress. Prepare **new language** on other aspects of your topic for the discussion.

There is an audio version of this extract from a student's presentation.

Now try this

 SPEAKING

Prepare a paragraph in answer to the following question.
- Was möchtest du nächstes Jahr machen?

Record yourself and listen back to hear how German you sound.

Future careers

Use the expressions on this page to include some high level language when you are talking about your future career.

Berufswünsche

Ich hoffe, ...   I hope ...

für ein großes Unternehmen zu arbeiten
to work for a large company

einen hohen Lohn zu verdienen
to earn a high wage

Chef zu werden
to become the boss

nicht in einer Fabrik zu arbeiten
not to work in a factory

(k)eine Schichtarbeit zu machen
(not) to do shift work

(nicht) draußen / im Freien zu arbeiten
(not) to work outside

von zu Hause aus zu arbeiten
to work from home

mit sympathischen Kollegen zusammen zu arbeiten
to work with nice colleagues

Lehrling zu sein
to be an apprentice

selbständig zu werden
to become independent

Infinitive expressions

Grammar page 96

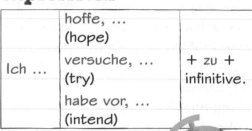

Ich ...	hoffe, ... (hope)	+ zu + infinitive.
	versuche, ... (try)	
	habe vor, ... (intend)	

Ich habe vor, ins Ausland zu reisen.
I intend to travel abroad.

Ich hoffe, viel Geld zu verdienen.
I hope to earn lots of money.

Ich fange an / beginne, an die Zukunft zu denken.
I am beginning to think of the future.

Ich versuche, einen Nebenjob zu finden.
I am trying to find a part-time job.

Worked example target C

What is important for these young people in their future careers?

1 Lothar ☐d☐   (a) travel
2 Ercan ☐e☐   (b) teamwork
3 Maria ☐   (c) outdoor work
4 Knut ☐   (d) excitement
5 Saskia ☐   (e) money

– Was findest du wichtig für deinen Beruf, Lothar?
– Routine ist nichts für mich. Ich suche etwas Spannendes.
– Und du, Ercan?
– Ich brauche unbedingt ein gutes Gehalt. Ich habe sehr teure Hobbys.

EXAM ALERT!

A number of Higher students did not recognise **Gehalt** (salary) and **etwas Spannendes** (something exciting). Don't be put off by extra letters at the end of familiar words: **spannend** = exciting.

This was a real exam question that a lot of students struggled with – **be prepared!**

- The first speaker states that 'routine isn't for me', so you can **infer** that (d) excitement is correct.
- Even if you don't know **Gehalt**, **teure Hobbys** (expensive hobbies), would lead you to (e) money.

Now try this target C

Listen to the rest of the recording and complete the above activity.

Jobs

Make sure you know both the male and female versions of the jobs listed below.

Berufe

Arzt / Ärztin	doctor
Zahnarzt / Zahnärztin	dentist
Apotheker/in	chemist
Bauer / Bäuerin	farmer
der Beamte / die Beamtin	civil servant
Briefträger/in	postman / woman
Elektriker/in	electrician
Feuerwehrmann	fireman
Fleischer / Metzger/in	butcher
Informatiker/in	IT specialist
Ingenieur/in	engineer
Kaufmann / Kauffrau	businessman / woman
Klempner/in	plumber
Krankenpfleger / Krankenschwester	nurse
Lkw-Fahrer/in	lorry driver
Mechaniker/in	mechanic
Polizist/in	police officer
Programmierer/in	programmer
Sekretär/in	secretary
Tischler/in	carpenter / joiner

Imperfect subjunctive modals

Impress with these expressions in your assessments. They are no more complicated than the modal in the present tense, but they will improve your speaking and writing!

Ich möchte Tierärztin werden.
I would like to become a vet.

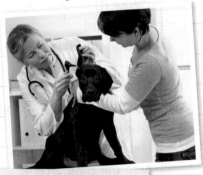

Note that in German the word for 'a' is not needed before the job.

Du könntest viel Geld verdienen.
You would be able to earn lots of money.

Du solltest versuchen, Arzt zu werden.
You should try to bcome a doctor

Worked example

Answer the questions in English.
1 How many sisters does Lars have? 2
2 What job does his older sister have?
3 Is Carmen a full-time sales assistant?
4 What does Lars say about his mother's job? Give **two** details.
5 What does Lars say about his father's job? Give **two** details.

– Ich stelle dir meine Familie vor. Meine ältere Schwester arbeitet als Krankenschwester und spielt unheimlich gern Tennis. Meine andere Schwester heißt Carmen.

Listening tips

- Read the questions BEFORE you listen.
- Watch out for questions requiring TWO pieces of information.
- If the answers are supposed to be in English, jotting down words in German won't help you!

You have to wait some time to get the answer to the first question. Don't jump to the conclusion that Lars only has **one** sister. Carry on listening and you will hear him mention **eine andere Schwester** (another sister).

Questions 4 and 5 ask for details about his parents' **jobs**. Do not give other information – it is **not** relevant.

Now try this

Listen to both parts of the recording and complete the above activity.

Job adverts

Make sure you're prepared with this vocabulary connected with job adverts.

Stellenanzeigen

Arbeit (f)	work
Arbeitsbedingungen (fpl)	work conditions
Arbeitsstunden (fpl)	hours of work
Bewerbung (f)	application
Euros pro Stunde	euros per hour
Firma (f)	company
Gehalt (n)	salary
Interview (n)	interview
Lebenslauf (m)	CV
Stelle (f)	job
Stellenangebote (mpl)	job vacancies
Stellenanzeige (f)	job advert
Unternehmen (n)	business
sich um eine Stelle bewerben	to apply for a job
Wir suchen Mitarbeiter.	We are looking for colleagues.
erfahren	experienced
qualifiziert	qualified
freundlich	friendly
hilfsbereit	helpful
verantwortlich	responsible

Genitive prepositions

The following all take the genitive case:

außerhalb	outside, beyond
statt	instead of
trotz	despite
während	during
wegen	due to, because of

(m) der Interviewer – statt des Interviewers

(der ➡ des + -s) instead of the interviewer

(f) die Pause – während der Pause

(die ➡ der) during the break

(n) das Gehalt – trotz des niedrigen Gehalts

(das ➡ des + -s) despite the low salary

(pl) die Arbeitsstunden – wegen der Arbeitsstunden

(die ➡ der) due to the working hours

To show possession, use the following:
der Job meines Vaters = my dad's job
der Chef der Firma = the firm's boss
der Bruder meiner Tante = my aunt's brother
das Ziel der Kinder = the children's aim

Worked example

Read these job adverts.

1 Für unser Team suchen wir erfahrene Verkäufer/innen. Gutes Gehalt und erstklassige Arbeitsbedingungen vorhanden.
2 Wir suchen qualifizierte Klempner, die uns bei den Kücheninstallationen helfen können.
3 Freundliche und geschäftige Tierarztpraxis sucht Hilfe.
4 Sie sind verantwortlich für die Online-Aktivitäten des Unternehmens. Schicken Sie uns Ihren Lebenslauf.

Which job would suit these people?

(a) Plumber 2   (c) Sales assistant
(b) Computer expert   (d) Vet

Reading tips

- Underline the jobs in the adverts and see how many of them you know.
- If you don't recognise the jobs vocabulary, look at what other CLUES are given in each advert, such as cognates and parts of the word being familiar.

If you didn't know that Klempner was a plumber, you could have worked it out, as it is somebody who could help with Kücheninstallationen (kitchen installations).

Now try this

Complete the above activity.

CV

You may want to include some details of a CV in your writing assessment.

Der Lebenslauf

Persönliche Daten (Personal details): ....
Geburtsdatum und -ort (Date of birth/place): ....

Schulausbildung (Education): ....
Berufsausbildung (Training): ....
Arbeitserfahrung (Work experience): ....
Sonstiges (Other): ....

Etwas, nichts, wenig + adjective

Try to include some of these higher level phrases.

viel Interessantes	a lot of interesting things
etwas Spannendes	something exciting
wenig Gutes	not much/little good
nichts Besonderes	nothing special

Worked example

Write a personal statement for your CV.

Mein Geburtsdatum ist der elfte August neunzehnhundertneunundneunzig. Ich wohne in Bath in Südwestengland und zurzeit besuche ich die St.-Thomas-Schule. Bevor ich nächstes Jahr auf die Uni gehe, möchte ich bei Ihnen arbeiten, um Erfahrungen zu sammeln.

AIMING HIGHER Ich bin am 11. August 1999 in Bath geboren. Ich war fünf Jahre lang in der St.-Thomas-Schule und ich habe in zehn Fächern gute Noten bekommen.

Für das Arbeitspraktikum habe ich eine Stelle in einem Gartenbetrieb gefunden. Ich interessiere mich sehr für Pflanzen und arbeite am liebsten im Freien.
Samstags bin ich immer im Hallenbad zu finden, wo ich kleinen Kindern das Schwimmen beibringe. Ich finde das toll, weil ich gut mit jungen Leuten auskomme.
Ich würde sagen, dass ich freundlich, geduldig, sportlich und ziemlich selbstbewusst bin. Ich bin aber auch ehrgeizig und möchte eines Tages eine erfolgreiche Karriere machen.

Writing strategies

The best answers use structures which show your level of knowledge and application.

- The first extract includes two important structures: bevor and um ... zu ....
- Use the headings from a CV to help you prepare for a presentation about yourself.
- You can also use the headings to write a biography of a famous person. Instead of ich bin / habe, use er / sie hat / ist.
- DON'T overcomplicate your work – stick to structures you are familiar with and get them (and the word order) right.
- DON'T overuse the same verbs: ist / war, hat / hatte and es gibt / gab are great, but don't use them all the time.
- DON'T write long lists – here the student writes he has good grades in ten subjects, rather than listing all the subjects individually.

Now try this

Copy the six headings from the CV at the top of the page and prepare a few sentences about each one.

Ich bin am ... in ... geboren.
Meine Lieblingsfächer sind ... , weil ...
Ich habe Erfahrung als ... Ich habe ...
In den Sommerferien habe/bin ich ...
Nächstes Jahr werde ich ...

Job application

Make sure you are familiar with letter-writing conventions, as you may meet them when reading a job application

Bewerbung für einen Job

Anbei finden Sie meinem Lebenslauf.
I enclose my CV.

Ich möchte vom 21. Juli bis 1. September arbeiten.
I would like to work from 21st July to 1st September.

Ich habe ausgezeichnete Sprachkenntnisse.
I have excellent language skills.

Letzten Sommer habe ich als Verkäuferin gearbeitet.
Last year I worked as a sales assistant.

Ich hoffe, später im Ausland Betriebswirtschaft zu studieren.
Later, I hope to study economics abroad.

Letter writing conventions

Sehr geehrter Herr X
Dear + man's name
Sehr geehrte Frau Y
Dear + woman's name
zu Händen von Z
For the attention of Z
Vielen Dank im Voraus
Many thanks in advance
Mit bestem Gruß
With best wishes
Mit freundlichen Grüßen
Yours sincerely
Alles Gute   All the best

Worked example

Read this letter about a job.

Ich möchte ab dem 1. Juli vier Wochen lang arbeiten. Ich habe ausgezeichnete Computerkenntnisse und ich spreche Türkisch und Englisch.

Letztes Jahr habe ich beim Verkehrsamt gearbeitet. Es hat mir gefallen, obwohl der Arbeitstag anstrengend war.

Ich hoffe, später im Ausland Marketing zu studieren.

Leyla can start work on …
(a) 21 May.
(b) 1 July. ✗
(c) 4 July.

EXAM ALERT!

Students who performed less well on this question didn't know the meaning of **Verkehrsamt** (tourist office) and **im Ausland** (abroad). Knowing key vocabulary is essential.

This was a real exam question that a lot of students struggled with – **be prepared!**

 ResultsPlus

Reading tips

- Pace yourself so you don't run out of time – this is a short letter, so don't spend too long pondering what a word means.

- Be prepared for vocabulary from a variety of topic areas to come up in any reading text. This one is a job application, but many of the words have little to do with jobs.

Now try this

Complete these sentences about the above letter.

1 Leyla's computer skills are …
   (a) excellent.   **(b)** good.   **(c)** average.

2 Leyla worked in …
   (a) a travel agent's.
   (b) a newsagent's.
   (c) a tourist information office.

3 Leyla found the working day …
   (a) tiring.   **(b)** frustrating.   **(c)** boring.

4 In the future Leyla hopes to …
   (a) study English.
   (b) work in a shop.
   (c) go abroad.

Job interview

Here you can prepare for an open interaction speaking task and role-play a job interview.

Das Bewerbungsgespräch

Ich will ein Jahr in Deutschland verbringen, um meine Deutschkenntnisse zu verbessern.
I would like to spend a year in Germany to improve my German.

Ich komme gut mit anderen Menschen aus.
I get on well with other people.

Ich arbeite gern in einem Team.
I like working in a team.

Im Sommer habe ich die Schule mit dem Abschlusszeugnis verlassen.
I left school in the summer with the leaving certificate.

Ich habe einen Erste-Hilfe-Kurs gemacht.
I did a First Aid course.

Letztes Jahr habe ich zwei Wochen bei einer internationalen Firma verbracht.
Last year I spent two weeks with an international firm.

Ich habe viel gelernt.
I learnt a lot.

Different words for 'you'

Sie / du

Familiar

du = 'you' to another young person, family member or friend, animal

ihr = 'you' plural of du

Formal

Sie = 'you' to adult(s), teacher(s), official(s)

Sie = singular and plural

Questions in a job interview

Wie sind die Arbeitsstunden?
What are the hours?

Gibt es gute Aufstiegsmöglichkeiten?
Are there good promotion prospects?

Wie viel Urlaub werde ich pro Jahr bekommen?
How much holiday will I get each year?

Worked example   59

CONTROLLED ASSESSMENT

Situation

You have applied to spend a year working in Germany. You are called for an interview.

Task

Your teacher is going to ask you about:

- why you want to spend a year abroad
- your education
- work experience
- your future plans.

Be prepared to ask questions in your discussion.

Listen to the interview.

In an open interaction you must ask at least **two** questions. Try to incorporate these naturally into the discussion, so you can benefit from taking the initiative. You will be penalised for not asking two questions.

- Notice how the student gains time by repeating the interviewer's question.

- He gives more than one answer to the question. Avoid really short answers – the longer you speak, the more control you have over the interview.

Now try this

Answer the questions about the job on the right in German.

- Warum willst du ein Jahr im Ausland verbringen?
- Welche Qualifikationen hast du?
- Hast du schon einmal ein Arbeitspraktikum gemacht?
- Was möchtest du in Zukunft machen?

Horizons-4-U

Specialists in jobs abroad for people of all ages

- Customer Services
- Human resources
- Sales and marketing
- Accountancy
- Translation

Opinions about jobs

The opinions on this page can equally well be applied to other topic areas – holidays, school, visits.

Meinungen über Arbeit

Angestellter / Angestellte	employee
Arbeitgeber (m)	employer
Bedingung (f)	condition
Besitzer (m)	owner
arbeitslos	unemployed
berufstätig	employed
ganztags	full-time
Ganztagsjob (m)	full-time job
gut / schlecht bezahlt	well / badly paid
Es gefällt mir (sehr).	I enjoy it (a lot).
Ich fühle mich wohl.	I feel comfortable.
Ich habe ein positives / negatives Gefühl.	I have a positive / negative feeling.

Giving opinions

Use the following to express an opinion.

Meiner Meinung nach sind die Arbeitsbedingungen prima.
In my opinion the terms and conditions are excellent.

Other words for 'to think':

finden · denken · meinen · glauben

Ich finde, dass manche Arbeitgeber gemein sind.
I think that many employers are mean.

Positives and negatives

Es ist ein großer Erfolg.	It is a big success.
Es bietet für jeden Geschmack etwas.	It offers something for every taste.
Es ist das Beste für mich.	It is the best for me.
Ich wäre gern noch länger geblieben.	I would have liked to stay longer.

Es ärgert mir sehr.	It really annoys me.
Das ist so ein Pech!	That is such bad luck.
Es ist eine große Enttäuschung.	It is a big disappointment.
Ich würde es niemandem empfehlen.	I wouldn't recommend it to anyone.
Ich würde das vermeiden.	I would avoid that.

Worked example

LISTENING 60 · **target B**

Listen. Are the statements positive or negative?

	🙂	🙁
1	X	
2		
3		

1 Meine neue Stelle ist ein großer Erfolg und macht mir besonders Spaß.

Understanding opinions

Many listening activities rely on you understanding the OPINION given. Listen to other clues such as the speaker's INTONATION to help you identify whether they are being POSITIVE or NEGATIVE.

Lots of positive words here, plus a happy-sounding speaker point you to the answer: positive.

Now try this

LISTENING 61 · **target B**

Listen to the remaining nine opinions and decide if they are positive or negative.

Watch out for the word **Probleme** in no. 4. Here it is linked with **trotz** (despite), so maybe it is a **positive** opinion after all?

Part-time work

When talking about part-time work, always use a range of vocabulary and structures, including weil, bevor, obwohl.

Der Nebenjob

Ich arbeite samstags als ...	I work Saturdays as a ...
Friseur / Friseurin	hairdresser
Gärtner/in	gardener
Kassierer/in	cashier
Kellner/in	waiter/waitress
Tellerwäscher	washer-upper
Verkäufer/in	sales assistant
Ich babysitte.	I babysit.

Ich trage Zeitungen aus.
I deliver newspapers.
Ich habe einen Ferienjob in einem Restaurant.
I've got a holiday job in a restaurant.
Ich habe einen Teilzeitjob in einer Autowerkstatt.
I've got a part-time job at a garage.
Ich verdiene 10 Euro pro Stunde.
I earn 10 euros an hour.

This / that, these / those, every, which

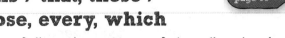
Grammar page 90

These follow the pattern of der, die, das (see page 49).

dieser	this / these
jener	that / those
jeder	every
welcher?	which?

	nom	acc	dat
masc	dieser	diesen	diesem
fem	diese	diese	dieser
neut	dieses	dieses	diesem
plural	diese	diese	diesen

(m acc) Welchen Job würdest du lieber machen?
Which job would you prefer to do?
(f acc) Ich finde jede Arbeit ermüdend.
I find every job tiring.
(n dat) Ich möchte in diesem Restaurant arbeiten.
I would like to work in this restaurant.

Worked example

WRITING

Write about your part-time job.

Jeden Samstag arbeite ich von neun bis dreizehn Uhr im Tanzstudio. Ich helfe beim Unterricht und verdiene dafür sechs Euro pro Stunde. Der Job gefällt mir sehr, weil Tanzen mein Lieblingshobby ist.

AIMING HIGHER

In den Sommerferien habe ich als Kellner in einer sehr beliebten Bar im Stadtzentrum gearbeitet. Am Anfang war ich sehr nervös, weil ich vorher noch nie in einem Restaurant gearbeitet hatte. Zwar war es sehr anstrengend, den Gästen den ganzen Tag die Getränke und Mahlzeiten zu servieren, aber es hat auch riesigen Spaß gemacht, besonders wenn die Gäste sympathisch waren.

CONTROLLED ASSESSMENT

These are some of the things to include in a piece of writing to help achieve a higher grade:
- excellent linking of the piece into a whole
- coherent and pleasant to read
- well-manipulated language which produces longer and fluent sentences.

This uses lots of exciting structures: imperfect, pluperfect, a filler zwar + inversion, both positive and negative opinions.

Now try this

WRITING

Describe your (real or imaginary) part-time job, in about 100 words.

Remember to include opinions!

My work experience

Talking about your work experience provides a good opportunity to use the past tense.

Das Betriebspraktikum

Ich habe im Büro / Reisebüro gearbeitet.
I worked in an office / travel agency.

Ich habe jeden Tag im Geschäft gearbeitet.
I worked every day in a shop.

Ich fand, das war eine positive/negative Erfahrung.
I found it a positive / negative experience.

Es war eine einmalige Gelegenheit, in einer Werkstatt zu arbeiten.
It was a unique opportunity to work in a workshop.

Ich habe eine Woche in einer Fabrik gearbeitet.
I spent a week working in a factory.

Saying 'somebody' and 'nobody'

JEMAND – somebody

Jemand hat mir geholfen.
Somebody helped me.

NIEMAND – nobody

Niemand möchte hier arbeiten.
Nobody wants to work here.

accusative = für jemanden / niemanden
dative = mit jemandem / niemandem

Worked example

Was hast du beim Betriebspraktikum gemacht?

Für mein Betriebspraktikum habe ich zwei Wochen in einem Büro gearbeitet, in dem mein Onkel als Informatiker arbeitet. Ich fand die Erfahrung toll, obwohl der Tag viel länger als ein typischer Schultag war.

AIMING HIGHER

Am ersten Tag musste ich an der Rezeption arbeiten und jemand hat mir beigebracht, wie das Computersystem funktioniert. Das war sehr kompliziert, aber glücklicherweise waren die Mitarbeiter alle sehr freundlich und geduldig. Niemand war böse, als ich ein paar Fehler gemacht habe. Ich denke, dass ich in Zukunft gern in einem Büro arbeiten würde. Mein Ziel ist es, eines Tages meine eigene Firma zu haben, damit ich keinen Chef habe.

- This is a solid piece of writing. It starts with a simple inversion and Time before Place sentence.
- It then continues with an **opinion** and the structure **obwohl** and comparison of school and working day.

To aim for a **top grade**, you have to go the extra mile and give plenty of details and facts, using a good range of **vocabulary, structures and tenses.**

Now try this

Look at the mind map and prepare an answer for each question.

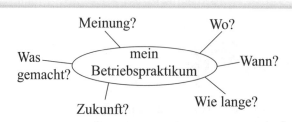

Meinung?   Wo?

Was gemacht? — mein Betriebspraktikum — Wann?

Zukunft?   Wie lange?

Work experience

When talking about work experience, try to include time expressions with past tense modals: Zuerst musste ich ... (First I had to ...) or Danach sollte ich ... (Afterwards I was supposed to ...).

Das Arbeitspraktikum

Ich habe ...	I ...
Aufgaben gemacht	did tasks
Kaffee gekocht	made coffee
kopiert	photocopied
Akten / Papiere sortiert	sorted files / paper
Anrufe beantwortet	answered calls
Kunden angerufen	phoned clients
Briefe geschrieben	wrote letters

Ich hatte viel / wenig / keinen Kontakt mit Kunden.
I had lots of / little / no contact with clients.

Es war faszinierend / ärgerlich.
It was fascinating / annoying.

Die Erfahrung war höchst interessant.
The experience was really interesting.

Ich war sehr / nicht beschäftigt.
I was very / not busy.

Adverbs of time

Usually, the verb must come second:

Dann habe ich den Kaffee gekocht.
Then I made coffee.

danach	afterwards	vorher	beforehand
dann	then	zuerst	first of all

With bevor and nachdem, the verb goes to the end:

Bevor ich mit der Aufgabe angefangen habe, musste ich mit dem Chef sprechen.
Before I started the task, I had to speak with the boss.

Nachdem ich die E-Mails gelöscht hatte, waren die Mitarbeiter nicht mehr so freundlich.
After I had deleted the emails, my colleagues weren't so friendly.

Worked example   target C

Silke is describing her work experience.
Put a cross in the correct box.

What did Silke most enjoy doing?
(a) Making phone calls. ☒
(b) Making coffee. ☐
(c) Typing letters. ☐

– Ich musste oft Kaffee kochen, aber am dritten Tag habe ich Kunden angerufen. Das hat mir besonders Spaß gemacht.

Any question with 'enjoy', 'like' or 'prefer' is looking for an opinion + activity, **not** just the activity the person did.

EXAM ALERT!

This question caused many students problems. They heard the distracter **Kaffee kochen** and did not wait for the correct answer: **am dritten Tag habe ich Kunden angerufen** which followed.

This was a real exam question that a lot of students struggled with – **be prepared!** ResultsPlus

Now try this   target C

Listen and complete the activity.

1 When was Silke's work experience?
 (a) Last week. (b) Last year.
 (c) Two years ago.
2 Where did she do her work experience?
 (a) In a hospital. (b) In a travel agent's.
 (c) In a school.

3 How did she feel at the end of the week?
 (a) Excited. (b) Tired. (c) Bored.
4 What does she want to be when she leaves school?
 (a) An engineer. (b) A tourist guide.
 (c) A police officer.

Dialogues and messages

Using a variety of verbs in the speaking and writing assessments will help make your work stand out

Gespräche und Mitteilungen

Ich bin gleich wieder da.	I'll be right back.
Kann ich etwas ausrichten?	Can I take a message?
Rufen Sie mich an.	Call me.
Augenblick.	Just a moment.
Warten Sie einen Moment.	Wait a moment.
Ich höre zu.	I'm listening.
Ich verbinde Sie.	I'll put you through.
Bis bald.	See you soon.
Bis später.	See you later.
Auf Wiederhören.	Goodbye. (on phone)
in Bezug auf …	relating to …
im Gespräch mit …	in conversation with …
simsen	to text
Mitteilung / SMS (f)	text message

Verbs for talking

Don't always use sagen (to say), but experiment with some of these alternatives.

anrufen	to phone
antworten / beantworten	to answer
befehlen	to order
beraten	to advise
beschreiben	to describe
besprechen / diskutieren	to discuss
empfehlen	to recommend
erklären	to explain
erzählen	to tell
fragen / eine Frage stellen	to ask (a question)
notieren	to note
reden	to talk
sprechen	to speak
wiederholen	to repeat

Worked example

Listen and choose the correct ending for each sentence.

1 Thomas is at … [c]
2 Thomas mustn't be … [ ]
3 He must take his … [ ]
4 He will travel by … [ ]

(a) worried.   (e) late.
(b) train.   (f) bus.
(c) the pool.   (g) school.
(d) white trainers. (h) black trainers.

- Frau Ingels am Apparat.
- Guten Tag, Frau Ingels, hier spricht Dieter. Kann ich bitte mit Thomas sprechen?
- Ach, tut mir leid, Thomas ist gerade im Hallenbad. Kann ich ihm etwas ausrichten?

EXAM ALERT!

Most students realised that for each question there were only two answers that were possible in the context.

Some students sensibly wrote the two possible choices on the paper during the 5-minute reading time before making their final decision on hearing the listening material.

> This was a real exam question that a lot of students struggled with – **be prepared!**
>
> ResultsPlus

Out of all the information you hear, the word **Hallenbad** (indoor pool) is what you need.

Now try this

mit der Bahn = mit dem Zug

Listen to the rest of the phone call and complete the above activity.

Language of the internet

The vocabulary here will help you become familiar with the language of the internet.

Internetsprache

mailen	to email
speichern	to save, store

Ich habe Internetanschluss auf dem Handy.
I have got internet access on my mobile.

Ich benutze das Internet, um für meine Freunde Videos freizugeben.
I use the internet to share videos.

Ich schreibe oft E-Mails.
I often write emails.

Ich chatte oft.
I often chat (online / MSN).

Ich lade (nie) Lieder herunter.
I (never) download songs.

Ich lade täglich Fotos hoch.
I upload photos every day.

Ich kann sehr schnell tippen.
I can type very fast.

Pluperfect tense

Grammar page 107

Pluperfect tense = HAD done something.

It is formed by using the imperfect form of haben / sein + past participle

Ich hatte es gedruckt.	I had printed it.
Sie war in den Urlaub gefahren.	She had gone on holiday.

Bildschirm (m)   Computer (m)   Drucker (m)

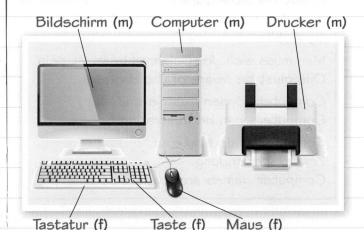

Tastatur (f)   Taste (f)   Maus (f)

Worked example

Read this text.

Simone und Anna, beide 16, arbeiten zweimal in der Woche in einem Internetcafé. Sie geben den Kunden Tipps im richtigen Umgang mit dem Internet, damit es nicht gefährlich wird: „Keine persönlichen Daten ins Netz", empfiehlt Simone. Früher hatte Anna so viel Zeit beim Chatten verbracht, dass sie ihr ganzes Taschengeld dafür im Internetcafé ausgegeben hat. Heute aber benutzt sie das Internet vor allem, um E-Mails an ihre Freunde zu schreiben.

Put a cross in the correct box.

Anna und Simone arbeiten ...

(a) täglich im Café. ☐
(b) regelmäßig im Café. ☒
(c) in den Ferien im Café. ☐

- The question here is **how often** Simone and Anna work in the café and you might spot the answer straight away: **zweimal in der Woche** (twice a week).

- **But zweimal in der Woche** is not given as an answer, so you have to work out that **täglich** = every day, so that isn't the answer.

- **Regelmäßig** = regularly, so that could be the answer and **in den Ferien** = in the holidays, which aren't mentioned.

- So you go back to (b) **regelmäßig** and put a cross

Now try this

Rat = advice, raten = to advise.

Answer these questions about the text above. Put a cross in the correct box.

1 Simones Hauptaufgabe im Café ist ...
(a) Getränke servieren. ☐   (b) Computer reparieren. ☐   (c) Rat geben. ☐

2 Chats im Internetcafé haben Anna ...
(a) viel Geld gekostet. ☐   (b) viel Zeit gespart. ☐   (c) viel Ärger gebracht. ☐

Internet pros and cons

Be prepared to give positive and negative views of the internet by using the phrases here.

Vorteile und Nachteile

Internetseite (f)	internet page
Kennwort/Passwort (n)	password
aktuell / weltweit	up to date / worldwide

Ich nutze das Internet, um Musik auf mein Handy herunterzuladen.
I use the internet to download music to my mobile.

Man muss sich der Gefahren bewusst sein.
One must be aware of the dangers.

Computer können frustrierend sein.
Computers can be frustrating.

Computerspiele sind eine Zeitverschwendung.
Computer games are a waste of time.

Using ob (whether)

Grammar page 95

ob = whether. It sends verb to the end:
Ich weiß nicht, ob er online ist.
I don't know whether he is online.

These conjunctions all send the verb to the end of the clause too:

dass	that	weil	because
obwohl	although	wenn	if

Das Internet ärgert mich, weil es so viele dumme Webseiten gibt.
I find the internet annoying because there are so many stupid websites.

Das Internet macht süchtig. The internet is addictive.

Worked example

WRITING

Write about the pros and cons of using a computer.

AIMING HIGHER Meiner Meinung nach sollten die Eltern dafür verantwortlich sein, dass ihre Kinder sich körperlich betätigen und nicht das Risiko eingehen, computersüchtig zu werden. Obwohl ich mir ein Leben ohne Computer nicht vorstellen kann, weiß ich schon, wann die Bildschirmzeit zu Ende sein sollte und wann ich etwas anderes und gesundes machen muss.

Aiming higher

- Use meiner Meinung nach + imperfect modal.
- A present modal reinforces knowledge of modal + infinitive.
- Use obwohl, which sends the verb to the end.
- Use higher level structures such as etwas anderes, sich vorstellen + dative pronoun.

Once you have written your text, check:
- **word order correct** (verb second or sent to the end by subordinating conjunction)
- **tenses secure** and make sense (don't hop from past to present to future without time markers or sensible meaning)
- **spelling accurate**, including adjective endings, genders and capital letters.

Now try this

WRITING

Answer the questions to write a paragraph of about 100 words about your online life and opinion.
- Wie oft bist du online?
- Was machst du online?
- Was ärgert dich online?
- Was findest du online gut?

Gender and plurals

When you are learning a German noun, always learn it with its word for 'the' (gender). All German words are masculine, feminine or neuter.

Der, die, das (the)

Every German noun is masculine
(m – der), feminine (f – die) or neuter
(n – das).

Der Mann ist groß.
The man is tall.

Die Frau ist klug.
The woman is clever.

Das Kind ist nervig.
The child is annoying.

Die Katzen sind süß.
The cats are cute.

	masc	fem	neut	pl
Nominative	der	die	das	die

If you don't know the gender of a word, you can look it up in a dictionary.

Mann [man] *m* man

Der, die, das as the subject

The definite articles der, die, das, die are used when the noun is the SUBJECT of the sentence. That means it is doing the action of the verb.

Der Lehrer spielt Fußball.
The teacher is playing football.

This is called the NOMINATIVE case.

Look at page 88 for more details of the cases in German.

Der, die, das as the object

BUT if the teacher becomes the OBJECT of the verb, i.e. is seen by someone else, then DER changes to DEN.

Ich sehe den Lehrer.   I see the teacher.

I = subject, as it is doing the seeing, and the teacher is the object, as he is being seen.

This is called the ACCUSATIVE case – die and das stay the same when used in this way.

	masc	fem	neut	pl
Accusative	den	die	das	die

Plurals

German nouns have different plurals. Not sure what they are? Check in a dictionary.

Mann [man] (¨er) *m* man

The part in brackets part tells you what to add to make the word plural. The umlaut before the –er ending tells you that an umlaut is added to the vowel before the ending, so the plural of **Mann** is **Männer**.

Now try this

Which definite article – **der**, **die** or **das**? Use a dictionary to find the gender and plural of these nouns.

(a) Anmeldung
(b) Fahrer
(c) Rührei
(d) Haltestelle
(e) Fernseher
(f) Brötchen

The gender is taken from the last word of compound nouns: der Abend + das Brot = das Abendbrot.

Cases 1

Prepositions such as durch (through) and zu (to) trigger a change in der, die or das, as they have to be followed by a specific case – the accusative, dative or genitive.

Changes to 'the'

	masc	fem	neut	pl
Nominative	der	die	das	die
Accusative	den	die	das	die
Dative	dem	der	dem	den
Genitive	des	der	des	der

Changes to 'a'

	masc	fem	neut	pl
Nominative	ein	eine	ein	keine
Accusative	einen	eine	ein	keine
Dative	einem	einer	einem	keinen
Genitive	eines	einer	eines	keiner

The genitive is not used that often, but it looks impressive if you can use it correctly!

keine – not a / no

Prepositions + accusative

Prepositions which trigger a change to the ACCUSATIVE case:

für	for
um	around
durch	through
gegen	against / towards
entlaug	along
bis	until
ohne	without

FUDGEBO = first letters of all accusative prepositions!

Ich kaufe ein Geschenk für einen Freund.
I am buying a present for a friend.

Geh um die Ecke.
Go round the corner.

Prepositions + dative

Prepositions which trigger a change to the DATIVE case:

aus	from		nach	after
außer	except		seit	since
bei	at, at the home of		von	from
gegenüber	opposite		zu	to
mit	with			

nach einer Weile
after a while

Fahr mit dem Bus.
Go by bus.

zu + dem = zum
zu + der = zur
bei + dem = beim

You need to add -n to the end of a plural masculine or neuter noun in the dative case:

mit meinen Freunden = with my friends.

Prepositions + genitive

Prepositions which trigger a change to the GENITIVE case:

laut	according to
trotz	in spite of
wegen	because of
laut der Zeitung	according to the newspaper
wegen des Wetters	because of the weather

You also need to add an -s to the end of a masculine or neuter noun in the genitive case.

Now try this

Translate these phrases into German by adding the preposition and changing the word for 'the' or 'a'.

(a) against the wall (die Mauer)
(b) except one child (ein Kind)
(c) despite the snow (der Schnee)
(d) after an hour (eine Stunde)
(e) to the shops (die Geschäfte – pl)
(f) without a word (ein Wort)
(g) during the summer (der Sommer)
(h) at the doctor's (der Arzt)

Cases 2

Movement TOWARDS or not? That is the key question with this group of prepositions, which can be followed by either the accusative or the dative case.

Dual case prepositions

an	at
auf	on
hinter	behind
in	in
neben	next to
über	over
unter	under
vor	in front of
zwischen	between

- If there is movement towards a place, these prepositions trigger a change to the ACCUSATIVE case.

  Ich gehe ins Haus. = I go into the house.

- If there is NO movement towards a place, these prepositions trigger a change to the DATIVE case.

  Ich bin im Haus. =
  I am in the house.

  in + das = ins
  in + dem = im

Verbs + accusative

Some verbs work with a preposition which is followed by the accusative case.

aufpassen auf	to look after
sich ärgern über	to be annoyed about
sich gewöhnen an	to get used to
sich streiten über	to argue about
sich erinnern an	to remember

sich freuen auf	to look forward to
warten auf	to wait for

Ich muss auf den Hund aufpassen.
I have to look after the dog.

Ich freue mich auf den Sommer.
I am looking forward to the summer.

Ich habe mich an die Arbeit gewöhnt.
I have got used to the work.

Prepositional phrases

Die Katze springt auf den Tisch. (acc)	The cat jumps onto the table.
Die Katze sitzt auf dem Tisch. (dat)	The cat is sitting on the table.
Ich surfe gern im Internet. (dat)	I like surfing the net.
Sie wohnt auf dem Land. (dat)	She lives in the countryside.
auf der linken Seite (dat)	on the left-hand side

As you can see here, where there is **no movement** the dual case preposition is generally followed by the **dative** case, and where there is a sense of **movement** it is followed by the **accusative**.

Now try this

Complete the sentences with the correct definite article ('the').

(a) Ich wohne an .... Küste (f).

(b) Er ärgert sich über .... Lärm (m).

(c) Was gibt es hinter .... Haus (n)?

(d) Wie finden Sie die Geschichte über .... Jungen (pl)?

(e) Die Nacht vor .... Hochzeit (f).

(f) Man muss zwischen .... Zeilen (pl) lesen.

(g) Denke an .... Namen (m sing).

(h) Erinnerst du dich an .... Person (f)?

Cases 3

Other groups of words, such as adjectives, also change according to case.

Words that follow the der, die, das pattern

These words follow the pattern of der, die, das:

dieser (this)   jeder (each)   jener (that)
mancher (some)   solcher (such)   welcher (which)

dieser Mann   this man

bei jeder Gelegenheit   at every opportunity

jedes Mal   every time

	masc	fem	neut	pl
Nominative	dieser	diese	dieses	diese
Accusative	diesen	diese	dieses	diese
Dative	diesem	dieser	diesem	diesen

Ways to use these words

dieses und jenes	this and that
in dieser Hinsicht	in this respect
jeder Einzelne	every individual
jeder Zweite	every other
zu jener Zeit / Stunde	at that time / hour
mancher Besucher	many a visitor / some visitors
Mit solchen Leuten will ich nichts zu tun haben.	I don't want to have anything to do with such people.
Welche Größe haben Sie?	What size are you?

Words that follow the ein pattern

These words follow the pattern of ein:

kein (not a)

mein (my)   unser (our)
dein (your)   euer (your, plural)
sein (his)   Ihr (your, polite)
ihr (her)   ihr (their)

	masc	fem	neut	pl
Nominative	kein	keine	kein	keine
Accusative	keinen	keine	kein	keine
Dative	keinem	keiner	keinem	keinen

ich habe keine Lust – I don't want to + infinitive with zu

meiner Meinung nach (dat) – in my opinion

Ways to use these words

keine Ahnung	no idea
mein Fehler	my mistake
gib dein Bestes	do your best
sein ganzes Leben	his whole life
ihr Ziel ist es …	it's her / their aim …
als unser Vertreter	as our representative
auf euren Handys	on your mobiles
Ihr Zeichen	your reference
für ihre Schularbeit	for their schoolwork

Now try this

Translate the sentences into English.

(a) Ich habe keine Lust, einkaufen zu gehen.

(b) Sie hat ihr ganzes Taschengeld für Kleidung ausgegeben.

(c) Solche Leute werden schnell unhöflich.

(d) Ich finde mein Leben langweilig.

(e) Dieses Mal fahren wir mit dem Zug.

(f) Seine Eltern sind arbeitslos.

(g) Solche Regeln finde ich dumm.

(h) Welches Buch liest du?

Adjective endings

Refer to these tables when you are preparing for your spoken and written assessments to check your adjective endings are CORRECT.

Adjective endings with the definite article 'the'

You can also use these endings after dieser (this), jener (that), jeder (each), mancher (many), solcher (such) and welcher (which). The endings are either -e or -en!

	masc	fem	neut	pl
Nominative	der kleine Hund	die kleine Maus	das kleine Haus	die kleinen Kinder
Accusative	den kleinen Hund	die kleine Maus	das kleine Haus	die kleinen Kinder
Dative	dem kleinen Hund	der kleinen Maus	dem kleinen Haus	den kleinen Kindern

Siehst du den kleinen Hund? Can you see the little dog?

Adjective endings with the indefinite article 'a'

You can also use these endings after kein (not a), mein (my), dein (your), sein (his), ihr (her / their), unser (our) and euer (your pl).

	masc	fem	neut	pl
Nominative	ein kleiner Hund	eine kleine Maus	ein kleines Haus	meine kleinen Kinder
Accusative	einen kleinen Hund	eine kleine Maus	ein kleines Haus	meine kleinen Kinder
Dative	einem kleinen Hund	einer kleinen Maus	einem kleinen Haus	meinen kleinen Kindern

Ich wohne in einem kleinen Haus. I live in a little house.

Adjective endings with no article

	masc	fem	neut	pl
Nominative	kleiner Hund	kleine Maus	kleines Haus	kleine Kinder
Accusative	kleinen Hund	kleine Maus	kleines Haus	kleine Kinder
Dative	kleinem Hund	kleiner Maus	kleinem Haus	kleinen Kindern

Kleine Kinder sind oft süß. Little children are often cute.

Many of these are similar to the definite articles: das Haus = kleines Haus, der Mann = großer Mann.

Now try this

Complete the sentences using the adjectives in brackets with their correct endings.

(a) Ich habe .... Deutschkenntnisse. (ausgezeichnet)

(b) Im Jugendklub kann ich .... Essen kaufen. (warm)

(c) Ich suche ein .... Bett. (preisgünstig)

(d) Die .... Lage war sehr praktisch. (zentral)

(e) Der Garten ist eine .... Raucherecke. (beliebt)

(f) Das ist eines der .... Lieder des Jahres. (meistverkauft)

(g) Letztes Wochenende gab es einen .... Sonntag. (verkaufsoffen)

(h) Stell keine .... Daten ins Netz. (persönlich)

Comparisons

To aim high, you will need to include comparatives and superlatives in your work, so always think of a way of making your assessments good, better ... best!

Formation

Add -er for the comparison, as in English (loud ➡ louder).

Add -(e)ste for the superlative 'most'.

Ich bin laut.   I am loud.

Ich bin lauter als du.
I am louder than you.

Ich bin die lauteste Person.
I am the loudest person.

- Adjectives are the same as adverbs, so you can compare how somebody does something very easily.

Ich schreie laut.	I shout loudly.
Ich schreie lauter als du.	I shout more loudly than you.
Ich schreie am lautesten.	I shout the loudest.

- Comparative and superlative adjectives have to agree with the noun they are describing.

die schöneren Ohrringe	the prettier earrings
der lustigste Junge	the funniest boy

Irregular comparatives

Some adjectives have small changes in the comparative and superlative forms.

alt	➡ älter	➡ älteste
old	older	oldest
jung	➡ jünger	➡ jüngste
young	younger	youngest
groß	➡ größer	➡ größte
big	bigger	biggest
gut	➡ besser	➡ beste
good	better	best
lang	➡ länger	➡ längste
long	longer	longest
hoch	➡ höher	➡ höchste
high	higher	highest

Gern, lieber, am liebsten

Use gern (like), lieber (prefer) and am liebsten (like most of all) to compare your likes and dislikes.

gern and lieber go after the verb:
Ich spiele gern Schach. ♥
I like playing chess.

Ich schwimme lieber. ♥♥
I prefer swimming.

Use am liebsten to start your sentence:
Am liebsten fahre ich Ski. ♥♥♥
Most of all I like skiing.

Lieblingssport – favourite sport
Lieblingsgruppe – favourite group

Now try this

Complete the sentences with a comparative or superlative form.

(a) Mathe ist viel .... als Chemie. (einfach)

(b) Mein Bruder ist .... als meine Schwester. (jung)

(c) Dieses Lied ist doch .... als der letzte Schlager. (gut)

(d) Meiner Meinung nach ist Physik .... als Chemie. (nützlich)

(e) Ich habe das .... Zimmer im Haus. (winzig)

(f) Das .... Fach in der Schule ist Informatik. (langweilig)

(g) Meine Stadt ist das .... Urlaubsziel in Deutschland. (beliebt)

(h) Letztes Jahr hatte ich die .... Noten in der Klasse. (schlecht)

Look at page 91 to check your endings.

Personal pronouns

Just like der, die, das, pronouns change depending on which case they are in – the nominative, accusative or dative case.

Pronouns

Pronouns = he, him, their, her, she, etc.

Nominative	Accusative	Dative
ich	mich	mir
du	dich	dir
er / sie / es	ihn / sie / es	ihm / ihr / ihm
wir	uns	uns
ihr	euch	euch
Sie / sie	Sie / sie	Ihnen / ihnen

- Use PRONOUNS to avoid repeating nouns.
  Ich mag Dieter, weil er nett ist.
  I like Dieter because he is nice.
- When a noun is the ACCUSATIVE OBJECT of the sentence, you need to use the ACCUSATIVE PRONOUN:
  Ich sehe ihn.   I see him.
- Use the correct pronoun after prepositions, depending on whether they take the accusative or dative case.
  bei mir (dat)   at my house
  für ihn (acc)   for him

Dative pronoun phrases

These expressions need a dative pronoun.

Es tut mir leid.	I am sorry.	Wie geht's dir / Ihnen?	How are you?
Es gefällt ihm.	He likes it.	Es geht uns gut.	We are well.
Es fällt mir schwer.	I find it difficult.	Es hilft ihnen.	It helps them.
Es tut ihr weh.	It hurts her.	Es scheint ihnen, dass ...	It seems to them that ...
Das schmeckt mir.	That tastes good.		
Sport macht ihr Spaß.	She finds sport fun.	Das ist uns egal.	We don't mind about that.

Sie or du?

Familiar

du = 'you' to another young person, family member/friend, animal

ihr = 'you' plural of du (more than one young person)

Formal

Sie = 'you' to adult(s), teacher(s), official(s)

Sie = singular and plural

Sie   du

Now try this

Choose the correct pronoun.

(a) Nina ist sympathisch, obwohl .... manchmal auch launisch ist.

(b) Es tut .... leid, aber ich kann nicht zur Party kommen.

(c) Seit wann geht es .... schlecht, Leon?

(d) Wir sind ins Theater gegangen, aber leider hat .... das Stück nicht gefallen.

(e) Mein Freund geht .... auf die Nerven, aber ich will nicht mit .... Schluss machen.

(f) Hast du Zeit, ... bei den Hausaufgaben zu helfen?

Word order

German word order follows rules – learn the rules and your sentences will be in the correct order.

Verb in second place

The VERB never comes first – it is always in second place!

① Ich   **②** fahre   **③** mit dem Auto.   **①** Jeden Tag   **②** fahre ich   **③** mit dem Auto.

Perfect tense

Form of haben / sein goes in second position:

① Gestern   **②** bin ich   **③** mit dem Auto   **④** gefahren.

> Remember:
> ich werde – I will / I am going to
> ich will – I want to

Future tense

Form of werden goes in second position:

① Morgen   **②** werde ich   **③** mit dem Auto   **④** fahren.

Modals

Form of modal goes in second position:

① Ich   **②** will   **③** mit dem Auto   **④** fahren.

Time – Manner – Place

A detail of transport counts as Manner, so put it after a Time expression, but before a Place.

(T) gestern / heute / letzte Woche / in Zukunft

(M) mit dem Zug / zu Fuß / mit meiner Familie

(P) nach London / in die Stadt / über die Brücke

(T) Ich fahre heute   **(M)** mit dem Zug   **(P)** nach Bonn.
Today I am going   by train   to Bonn.

Linking words

No word order change here!

aber   but   oder   or
denn   because   und   and

Ich spiele gern Tennis und ich fahre gern Rad.
I like playing tennis and I like cycling.

Ich esse gern Pommes, aber ich esse nicht gern Bratkartoffeln.
I like eating chips but I don't like roast potatoes.

Now try this

Order the sentences following the above rules.

(a) fahre / ich / ins Ausland / gern
(b) Verkehrsamt / findet / Informationen / beim / man
(c) gesund / ich / normalerweise / esse
(d) sehen / manchmal / Filme / wir / im Jugendklub
(e) arbeiten / ich / im Sportzentrum / möchte / im Juli
(f) habe / gearbeitet / ich / in einem Büro / letztes Jahr
(g) gehe / ins Kino / mit meiner Mutter / morgen / ich

> Try to invert your sentences by starting with a time expression rather than **ich, du**, etc.

Conjunctions

You will be expected to use plenty of conjunctions like weil, wenn and als in your spoken assessment – and you will HAVE to show you can use them correctly.

Verb to the end

Weil (because) sends the verb ➡ to the END.

Ich rede über Beyonce, weil sie meine Lieblingssängerin ist.
I am talking about Beyonce because she is my favourite singer.

Ich gehe nicht gern ins Kino, weil das zu teuer ist.
I don't like going to the cinema because it is too expensive.

All these conjunctions also send the verb to the end of the clause, just like weil.

als	when (one occasion, past tense)	nachdem	after
bevor	before	ob	whether
bis	until	obwohl	although
da	because / since	während	while
		was	what
damit	so that	wie	how
dass	that	wenn	when / if (present or future)

Perfect tense

- In the PERFECT tense, the form of haben / sein is LAST in a clause.

  Ich kann nicht zur Party kommen, obwohl ich meine Hausaufgaben gemacht habe.
  I can't come to the party although I have done my homework.

- Watch out for the VERB, COMMA, VERB structure.

  Als ich klein war, habe ich viel im Garten gespielt.
  When I was small I played in the garden a lot.

Future tense and modals

- In the FUTURE tense, it is the form of werden which goes last.

  Da ich nach Afrika reisen werde, muss ich zum Arzt.
  Because I am going to travel to Africa, I have to go to the doctor.

- With MODAL verbs, it is the modal itself which is last in the clause.

  Ich bin immer glücklich, wenn ich ins Konzert gehen darf.
  I am always happy when I am allowed to go to the concert.

Form of modal ➡ right to the end
Form of haben / sein in the perfect tense ➡ right to the end

Now try this

Join these sentences with the subordinating conjunction in brackets.

(a) Ich habe bei meiner Großmutter gewohnt. Meine Mutter war im Krankenhaus. (während)
(b) Ich bin ins Café gegangen. Ich habe ein T-Shirt gekauft. (nachdem)
(c) Ich war in Spanien im Urlaub. Ich habe einen neuen Freund kennengelernt. (als)
(d) Er ist sehr beliebt. Er ist nicht sehr freundlich. (obwohl)
(e) Ich werde für eine neue Gitarre sparen. Ich finde einen Nebenjob. (wenn)
(f) Ich bin froh. Ich habe gute Noten in der Schule bekommen. (dass)
(g) Ich muss meine Eltern fragen. Ich darf ins Konzert gehen. (ob)
(h) Er hat mir gesagt. Er will mit mir ins Kino gehen. (dass)

More on word order

There are a few more structures here which you should try and fit into your work to improve your writing and speaking. They also affect word order, so be careful!

Using um ... zu ...

Um ... zu ... means 'in order to' and is used in German where we might just say 'to'. It requires an infinitive verb at the end of the clause.

Ich trage Zeitungen aus, um Geld zu verdienen. [*infinitive verb*]
I deliver newspapers, (in order) to earn money.

- Only use um ... zu ... where you would say 'in order to' in English, even if you drop the 'in order' bit.
- The verb after um ... zu ... is always in the infinitive and at the END.
- Add a comma before um.

ohne ... zu ... = without, and works in the same way.
Ich bin in die Schule gegangen, ohne ihn zu sehen. I went to school without seeing him.

Infinitive expressions

These expressions with zu need an infinitive.

ich ... (I ...)	hoffe, ... (hope) versuche, ... (try) beginne / fange an, ... (begin) habe vor, ... (intend) nutze die Chance (use the opportunity)	+ zu + infinitive

Ich hoffe, Deutsch zu studieren.
I hope to study German.

Ich versuche, einen guten Job zu bekommen.
I am trying to get a good job.

Separable verbs have the zu after the prefix.
Ich habe vor, fernzusehen.
I intend to watch TV.

See page 74.

Relative pronouns

Relative pronouns send the verb to the end of the clause.

They are used to express WHO or THAT or WHICH.

m Der Mann, der im Café sitzt, ist Millionär.
The man who is sitting in the café is a millionaire.

f Die Katze, die unter dem Tisch schläft, ist sehr süß.
The cat that is sleeping under the table is very sweet.

n Das Mädchen, das einen roten Rock trägt, singt in einer Band.
The girl who's wearing a red skirt sings in a band.

Now try this   LISTENING 66

1 Combine the sentences with **um ... zu ...** .
   (a) Ich fahre nach Italien – ich besuche meine Verwandten.
   (b) Ich gehe zum Sportzentrum – ich nehme 5 Kilo ab.

2 Combine the sentences with **zu**.
   (a) Ich versuche – ich helfe anderen.
   (b) Ich habe vor – ich gehe auf die Uni.

3 Combine the sentences with a relative pronoun.
   (a) Das ist das Geschäft. Das Geschäft hat Sommerschlussverkauf.
   (b) Hier ist eine Kellnerin. Die Kellnerin ist sehr unhöflich.

The answers are also available via the audio link.

The present tense

There are regular and irregular present tense verbs for you here, but look at page 102 for the super-irregular verbs haben (to have) and sein (to be).

Present tense regular

Verbs change according to who is doing the action, just like in English: I drink ➡ he drinks.

The present tense describes what is happening now and can be translated 'drink' or 'am drinking'.

machen – to do / to make		⬅ *infinitive verb*
ich	mache	I do / make
du	machst	you do / make
er / sie / es	macht	he / she / it does / makes
wir	machen	we do / make
ihr	macht	you do / make
Sie / sie	machen	they / you do / make

wir / sie / Sie forms = same as infinitive

- The present tense is used to describe what are you DOING now or what you DO regularly.
- Present tense time expressions include:

  jetzt (now)   heute (today),
  im Moment   dienstags
  (at the moment)   (on Tuesdays).

- You can use the present tense with a time phrase to indicate the FUTURE.

  Morgen fahre ich nach London.
  Tomorrow I am going to London.

Present tense vowel changes

Some verbs have a vowel change in the du and er / sie / es forms of the present tense, but they still have the same endings (-e, -st, -t, etc.).

infinitive verb

geben – to give			⬅
ich	gebe	wir	geben
du	gibst	ihr	gebt
er / sie /es	gibt	Sie / sie	geben

vowel change

nehmen – to take	
ich	nehme
du	nimmst
er / sie / es	nimmt

essen – to eat	
ich	esse
du	isst
er / sie / es	isst

schlafen – to sleep	
ich	schlafe
du	schläfst
er / sie / es	schläft

Sie schläft.

Now try this

Complete the sentences with the correct form of the present tense verb in brackets.

(a) Ich .... gern Musik. (hören)

(b) Meine Schwester .... im eigenen Zimmer. (schlafen)

(c) Ihr .... montags schwimmen, oder? (gehen)

(d) .... du gern Wurst mit Senf? (essen)

(e) Wir .... nie mit dem Auto. (fahren)

(f) Was .... Sie in den Sommerferien? (machen)

(g) .... es eine Ermäßigung für Senioren? (geben)

(h) Mein Bruder .... heute im Bett, weil er krank ist. (bleiben)

More on verbs

To aim for a higher grade, try to include separable and reflexive verbs in your speaking and writing assessments.

Separable verbs

These verbs have two parts: a prefix + the main verb. They go their separate ways when used in a sentence.

← →

Ich sehe oft fern.   I often watch TV.

Ich wasche nicht so gern ab.
I don't much like washing up.

abwaschen	to wash up
aufwachen	to wake up
aussteigen	to get off
einsteigen	to get on
fernsehen	to watch TV
herunterladen	to download
hochladen	to upload
umsteigen	to change (trains, trams, buses)

Make sure you can use separable verbs in all the tenses.

PRESENT: Ich steige in Ulm um.
I change in Ulm.

PERFECT: Ich bin in Ulm umgestiegen.
I changed in Ulm.

Separable verbs form the past participle as one word with -ge- sandwiched in the middle: **abgewaschen** (washed up), **ferngesehen** (watched TV).

FUTURE: Ich werde in Ulm umsteigen.
I will change in Ulm.

MODALS: Ich muss in Ulm umsteigen.
I have to change in Ulm.

Reflexive verbs

Reflexive verbs need a reflexive pronoun – mich, dich, etc.

sich freuen – to be happy / pleased	
ich freue mich	wir freuen uns
er / sie / es freut sich	ihr freut euch
du freust dich	Sie / sie freuen sich

Note that sich never has a capital letter.
sich freuen auf ... (acc) – to look forward to ...

sich amüsieren	to enjoy oneself
sich befinden	to be located
sich entscheiden	to decide
sich erinnern an	to remember
sich langweilen	to be bored
sich interessieren für	to be interested in

Ich interessiere mich für Geschichte.
I am interested in history.

All reflexive verbs use **haben** in the perfect tense.
Er hat sich rasiert.   He shaved.
Wir haben uns gelangweilt. We were bored.

Now try this

1 Translate the sentences into German.
   (a) I watch TV. I watched TV.
   (b) I change trains at six o'clock. I changed trains at six o'clock.
   (c) I download music. I will download music.
   (d) I washed up. I have to wash up.

2 Complete the sentences with the correct reflexive pronoun.
   (a) Ich erinnere .... kaum an meinen Vater.
   (b) Wir interessieren .... für Mode.
   (c) Habt ihr .... im Jugendklub gelangweilt?
   (d) Meine Schule befindet .... am Stadtrand.

Commands

Use this page to help you give commands and orders accurately.

Sie commands

Swap the present tense round so the verb comes before the pronoun:

Sie hören (you listen) ➡
Hören Sie bitte! Listen!

Schreiben Sie das auf Deutsch auf.
Write that in German.

Geben Sie keine Kontaktdaten an.
Don't give any contact details.

- Separable verbs separate and the prefix goes to the end of the sentence.
  Tauschen Sie nicht Ihre Telefonnummer aus.
  Don't swap your phone number.
- Sein (to be) is irregular.
  Seien Sie nicht aggressiv.
  Don't be aggressive.
- Other words you may come across in commands:

Gas weg!	Reduce your speed!
Gefahr!	Danger!
Warnung!	Warning!
Achtung!	Attention! / Watch out!
Vorsicht!	Be careful!
Verboten!	Forbidden!
Kein Eintritt! ⊖	Keep off!
Nicht betreten!	No entry!
Ausfahrt freihalten!	Keep exit clear!
! Lebensgefahr!	Danger of death!
Privatgrundstück	Private land

Du commands

Use the present tense du form of the verb minus the -st ending.

gehen ➡ du gehst ➡ du ge~~hst~~ ➡ Geh!

Hab viel Spaß. Have a lot of fun.

Bleib anonym. Stay anonymous.

Triff niemanden allein.
Don't meet anyone on your own.

Beleidige andere nicht.
Don't insult others.

Such dir einen Spitznamen aus.
Choose a nickname.

This is a separable verb so it splits.

Some verbs are irregular in the present tense, so make sure you get it right for a command.

essen – to eat	➡	Iss! – Eat!	
fahren – to drive	➡	Fahr! – Drive!	
geben – to give	➡	Gib her! – Give!	
lassen – to leave	➡	Lass das! – Leave that!	
nehmen – to take	➡	Nimm! – Take!	

Now try this

What is this sign asking dog owners to do?

Liebe Hundehalter,
bitte achten Sie auf
ihre Lieblinge und
benutzen Sie
Grüflächen und
Wege nicht als
Hundetoilette

Vielen Dank!

Present tense modals

Modal verbs need another verb in the infinitive form, e.g. gehen (to go), kaufen (to buy). The modal verb comes second in the sentence, while the infinitive is shifted to the very end.

Können (to be able to)

ich / er / sie	kann
du	kannst
sie / wir / Sie	können

Ich kann nicht schwimmen. I can't swim.

Müssen (to have to / must)

ich / er / sie	muss
du	musst
sie / wir / Sie	müssen

Du musst deine Hausaufgaben machen.
You have to do your homework.

Wollen (to want to)

ich / er / sie	will
du	willst
sie / wir / Sie	wollen

Er will nicht umsteigen.
He doesn't want to change (trains).

Dürfen (to be allowed to)

ich / er / sie	darf
du	darfst
sie / wir / Sie	dürfen

Wir dürfen in die Disko gehen.
We are allowed to go to the disco.

Sollen (to ought to)

ich / er / sie	soll
du	sollst
sie / wir / Sie	sollen

Germans far more often use the imperfect tense of sollen to express the sense of 'should' or 'ought'

Ich sollte meine Großeltern besuchen.
I should visit my grandparents.

Mögen (to like to)

The present tense of mögen no longer tends to be used in the present tense with another verb to express liking. Instead, the conditional form is far more likely to be used in the sense of 'would like' or 'like'.

ich / er / sie	möchte
du	möchtest
sie / wir / Sie	möchten

Sie möchte Rollschuhlaufen gehen.
She likes to go rollerblading.

The negative form still uses the present tense form, however:

Ich mag nicht ins Kino gehen.
I don't like to go to the cinema.

Now try this

Write modal sentences using the verbs given in brackets.

(a) Ich gehe um einundzwanzig Uhr ins Bett. (müssen)
(b) In der Schule raucht man nicht. (dürfen)
(c) Du deckst den Tisch. (sollen)
(d) Hilfst du mir zu Hause? (können)
(e) Ich fahre in den Ferien Ski. (wollen)
(f) Ich sehe am Wochenende fern. (mögen)
(g) Ich löse das Problem nicht. (können)

> Note that separable verbs come together as infinitives: ich sehe fern = fernsehen.

Imperfect modals

Using modals and an infinitive in different tenses is a great way of incorporating a variety of tenses into your work.

Imperfect modals

Infinitive: können – to be able to

Present tense:
ich kann + infinitive at end = I can ... ➡

Imperfect tense:
ich konnte + infinitive at end = I was able to ...

Ich konnte nicht mehr warten.
I couldn't wait any more.

infinitive at the end

The endings change, depending on the subject of the verb.

ich	konnte
du	konntest
er / sie / man	konnte
wir	konnten
Sie / sie	konnten
ihr	konntet

Other modals in the imperfect

- These modals work in the same way as konnte – just add the correct ending.
- There are no umlauts on imperfect tense modals.

müssen	➡ musste	had to
wollen	➡ wollte	wanted to
dürfen	➡ durfte	was allowed to
sollen	➡ sollte	was supposed to
mögen	➡ mochte	liked

Was musstet ihr gestern in Mathe machen?
What did you have to do in maths yesterday?

Er wollte doch nur helfen.
He only wanted to help.

Sie durfte ihn nicht heiraten.
She wasn't allowed to marry him.

Du solltest eine Tablette nehmen.
You should take a pill.

Subjunctive modals (Higher)

Add an umlaut to konnte and mochte and you have the subjunctive. This allows you to talk about things you COULD / WOULD do.

imperfect	➡	subjunctive	
konnte	➡	könnte (could)	+ infinitive
mochte	➡	möchte (would like)	

The subjunctive has the same structure as imperfect modals with the infinitive at the end.

Möchtest du ins Kino gehen?
Would you like to go to the cinema?

Das Schwimmbad könnte geschlossen sein.
The swimming pool could be closed.

Now try this

1. Rewrite these sentences with an imperfect tense modal.
   (a) Ich mache Hausaufgaben. (müssen)
   (b) Sie helfen mir nicht. (können)
   (c) Er kauft eine neue Hose. (wollen)
   (d) Wir räumen das Zimmer auf. (sollen)
   (e) In der Schule kaut man nie Kaugummi. (dürfen)
   (f) Alle Schüler bleiben bis sechzehn Uhr. (müssen)

2. Rewrite these with a subjunctive modal.
   (a) Es wird schwierig. (können)
   (b) Ich zahle das Geld auf mein Konto ein. (mögen)

The perfect tense 1

The perfect tense is the main past tense in German. Using it is essential if you are aiming for a top grade.

The perfect tense

- Use the perfect tense to talk about something you have done in the PAST.
- The perfect tense is made up of TWO PARTS:

the correct form of HABEN or SEIN + past participle at the end.

Ich habe Musik gehört.
I listened to music.

Past participles generally start with ge-.

spielen	➡	gespielt (played)
lachen		gelacht (laughed)
fahren	➡	gefahren (drove)

Hast du den Film gesehen?
Have you seen the film?

The perfect tense – haben

Most verbs use haben (to have) in the perfect tense:

form of haben + sentence + past participle at the end.

ich habe	
du hast	gekauft (bought)
er / sie / es hat	gemacht (made)
wir haben	besucht (visited)
ihr habt	gesehen (seen)
Sie / sie haben	

Er hat im Reisebüro gearbeitet.
He worked at the travel agency.

Wir haben Frühstück gegessen.
We ate breakfast.

The perfect tense – sein

Some verbs of movement use sein (to be) to make the perfect tense:

form of sein + sentence + past participle at the end.

ich bin	
du bist	gegangen (went)
er / sie / es ist	geflogen (flew)
wir sind	gefahren (drove)
ihr seid	geblieben (stayed)
Sie / sie sind	

Sie ist zu Fuß gegangen. She went on foot.

Ich bin nach Freiburg gefahren.
I went to Freiburg.

There are some verbs that use **sein** in the perfect tense where there is no apparent movement: **bleiben** is such an example.

Now try this

Write these sentences in the perfect tense.

(a) Ich kaufe eine Jacke.
(b) Wir fliegen nach Ungarn.
(c) Ich sehe meinen Freund.
(d) Lena und Hannah gehen in die Stadt.
(e) Ich besuche meine Tante.
(f) Ich bleibe im Hotel.
(g) Was isst du zu Mittag?
(h) Am Samstag hört er Musik.

Put the form of **haben / sein** in **second** position and the past participle at the end of the sentence.

The perfect tense 2

Spotting past participles will help you to identify when a text is in the past tense – but watch out for the hidden ge- in separable verbs, such as ferngesehen (watched TV).

Regular past participles

- Begin with ge-.
- End in -t.

Remove -en from the infinitive and replace with –t: machen ➡ macht ➡ gemacht

Das hat ihr Spaß   That was fun
gemacht.   for her.

Some exceptions

Verbs starting with be-, emp- or ver- do not add ge- for the past participle.

Ich habe ...	I ...
besucht	visited
empfohlen	recommended
vergessen	forgot
verloren	lost

Separable verbs add **ge-** between the prefix and the main verb.
hochgeladen   uploaded   heruntergeladen   downloaded

Irregular past participles

There are no rules for forming these past participles – but here are some common ones to learn.

Ich habe ...	gegessen	ate
	getrunken	drank
	genommen	took
	geschlafen	slept
	geschrieben	wrote
	gesungen	sang
	getragen	wore / carried
	getroffen	met
	gestanden	stood
Ich bin ...	gerannt	ran
	geschwommen	swam
	gewesen	have been
	gestiegen	climbed
	gestorben	died
	geworden	became

Word order

- The past participle goes at the END of the sentence and the form of haben or sein is in SECOND position.

❶ Er   ❷ ist   ins Kino   ❸ gegangen.
He went to the cinema.

❶ Am Montag   ❷ habe ich   Fußball   ❸ gespielt.
I played football on Monday.

- When the verb has already been sent to the end by a conjunction such as weil (because) or als (when), the part of haben or sein comes AFTER the past participle.

Ich war dankbar, weil er mein Portemonnaie gefunden hat.
I was grateful because he found my purse.

Als er ankam, war er erschöpft.
When he arrived, he was exhausted.

Now try this

Complete the sentences with the correct past participle of the verb in brackets.

(a) Ich habe zu viele Kekse .... (essen)
(b) Haben Sie gut .... ? (schlafen)
(c) Wir haben uns am Bahnhof .... (treffen)
(d) Ich war krank, weil ich den ganzen Tag .... habe. (stehen)
(e) Ich weiß, dass du .... bist. (umsteigen)

(f) Warum hast du die E-Mail .... ? (schreiben)
(g) Ich habe ihr .... , dass sie nicht mitkommen sollte. (empfehlen)
(h) Ich war sehr traurig, als er .... ist. (sterben)

The imperfect tense

If you are telling a story about the past or recounting a series of events in the past, use the imperfect tense.

Forming the imperfect tense

- Take the infinitive, e.g. hören (to hear).
- Take off the final -en ➡ hören = hör.
- Add these endings:

ich hörte	I heard / was hearing
du hörtest	you heard / were hearing
er / sie / man hörte	he / she / one heard / was hearing
wir hörten	we heard / were hearing
ihr hörtet	you heard / were hearing
Sie / sie hörten	they / you heard / were hearing

Ich hörte gar nichts.
I didn't hear a thing.

Sie spielten drei Jahre lang mit der Gruppe.
They played for three years with the group.

'To have' and 'to be' in the imperfect

HABEN

ich hatte	I had
du hattest	you had
er / sie / man hatte	he / she / one had
wir hatten	we had
ihr hattet	you had
Sie / sie hatten	they / you had
Ich hatte Glück.	I was lucky.

SEIN

ich war	I was
du warst	you were
er / sie / man war	he / she / one was
wir waren	we were
ihr wart	you were
Sie / sie waren	they / you were
Es war teuer.	It was expensive.

> Don't forget to use the imperfect modals – see page 101.

Irregular verbs

- Some verbs have irregular stems in the imperfect tense.
- Add the same basic endings as above to the irregular stems on the right:

  Ich ging – wir gingen (I went – we went)

  Ich fuhr – wir fuhren (I drove – we drove)

Im Stück ging es um eine Beziehung.
The play was about a relationship.

Die Kinder sahen blass aus.
The children looked pale.

Es fand in Hamburg statt.
It took place in Hamburg.

gehen ➡	ging	went
fahren ➡	fuhr	drove
finden ➡	fand	found
kommen ➡	kam	came
nehmen ➡	nahm	took
sehen ➡	sah	saw
sitzen ➡	saß	sat
stehen ➡	stand	stood
tut weh ➡	tat weh	hurt

Es gab is an impersonal verb and so does not change.

Es gab ein Haus.	There was a house.
Es gab zwei Häuser.	There were two houses.

Now try this

Put these sentences into the imperfect tense.

(a) Sie hat Angst.
(b) Es ist hoffnungslos.
(c) Wo tut es dir weh?
(d) Hörst du das?
(e) Plötzlich kommt uns der Mann entgegen.
(f) Das ist eine Überraschung, nicht?
(g) Es ist niemand zu Hause.
(h) Sie spielen gern Tischtennis.

> Spielen is a regular verb like hören.

The future tense

As well as using the future tense, you can also express future intent using the present tense. Use this page to check you can do both!

The future tense

Use the future tense to talk about things you WILL do or that WILL happen in the future:

form of werden (to become) + sentence + infinitive at the end.

ich werde	
du wirst	vergessen (forget)
er / sie / man wird	spielen (play)
wir werden	holen (collect)
ihr werdet	klopfen (knock)
Sie / sie werden	

Word order in the future tense

Form of werden in second position

Nächste Woche werde ich in den Urlaub fahren.

Ich werde erfolgreich sein.
I will be successful.

Wie groß wirst du werden?
How tall will you get?

Morgen wird es kalt sein.
It will be cold tomorrow.

Werden sie auf die Uni gehen?
Will they go to university?

Ich bin froh, dass du zu Besuch kommen wirst.
I am happy that you will come to visit.

Reflexive and separable verbs

- Reflexive verbs – add the pronoun after part of werden:

  Ich werde mich schnell rasieren.
  I will shave quickly.

- Separable verbs – stay together at the end of the sentence:

  Er wird das Lied herunterladen.
  He will download the song.

Present tense with future intent

You can use the present tense to express what you are GOING TO do. Include a time marker to make sure the intent is based in the future.

morgen	tomorrow
übermorgen	the day after tomorrow
nächste Woche	next week

Nächsten Sommer fahren wir nach Amerika.
We are going to America next summer.

Now try this

Rewrite the sentences in the future tense with **werden**.

(a) Ich gewinne das Spiel.
(b) Wir gehen in den Freizeitpark.
(c) Sie mieten eine große Wohnung.
(d) Ihr habt große Schwierigkeiten.
(e) Er besteht die Prüfung.
(f) Nächste Woche ziehen wir um.
(g) Schminkst du dich heute?
(h) Ich ziehe mich um sechs Uhr an.

The conditional

The conditional is very similar in structure to the future tense and using it will improve your writing and speaking.

Conditional

Use the conditional to talk about things you WOULD do or that WOULD happen in the future: part of würde (would) + sentence + infinitive at the end.

ich würde	
du würdest	
er / sie / man würde	+ infinitive
wir würden	
ihr würdet	
Sie / sie würden	

Ich würde gern nach Italien fahren.
I would like to go to Italy.

Würden Sie lieber Geschäftsmann oder Klempner werden?
Would you rather become a businessman or a plumber?

Würdest du je rauchen?
Would you ever smoke?

Man würde nie ein Auto kaufen.
One would never buy a car.

> würde sein = wäre – would be
> würde haben = hätte – would have
> es würde geben = es gäbe – there would be

Using wenn

- You often use wenn (if) with the conditional tense.
- Remember: verb – comma – verb!

Wenn ich reich wäre, würde ich keine Designerkleidung kaufen.
If I were rich, I wouldn't buy designer clothes.

Wenn sie ein Vorstellungsgespräch hätte, würde sie rechtzeitig ankommen.
If she had an interview, she would arrive on time.

Making requests

Use the conditional tense to make a request for something you WOULD like.

Ich möchte Pommes essen.
I would like to eat chips.

The plural form adds -n.

wir möchten
we would like

sie hätten gern
they would like
to have

> Sie hätte gern ein neues Handy.
> She would like a new mobile.

Now try this

Rewrite these sentences using the conditional.

(a) Ich gehe gern ins Theater.
(b) Er kommt nie spät an.
(c) Wir nehmen nie Drogen.
(d) Helfen Sie mir bitte?
(e) Zum Geburtstag bekommt sie am liebsten Geld.
(f) Nächstes Jahr heiraten sie vielleicht.
(g) Wenn Latein Pflicht ist, gehe ich auf eine andere Schule.
(h) Wenn ich das mache, gibt es Krach mit meinen Eltern.

The pluperfect tense

The pluperfect tense is used to say you HAD done something. Use it to aim for a top grade!

Forming the pluperfect

- Use the pluperfect tense to talk about events which HAD happened.
- It is made up from the IMPERFECT of haben or sein + past participle.

ich hatte	
du hattest	Pause gemacht
er / sie / man hatte	(I had had a break)
wir hatten	Freunde gesehen
ihr hattet	(I had seen friends)
sie / Sie hatten	

ich war	
du warst	Ski gefahren
er / sie / man war	(I had been skiing)
wir waren	zu Hause geblieben
ihr wart	(I had stayed at
sie / Sie waren	home)

Haben or sein?

- Some participles take haben and some sein. The same rules apply as for the perfect tense.

  Sie hatte kein Wort gesagt.
  She had not said a word.

ich hatte	angefangen / begonnen (I had begun)
	gearbeitet (worked)
	gebracht (brought)
	eingeladen (invited)
	erreicht (reached)
	geholt (fetched)
	gelogen (lied)

Er war nicht gekommen.   He had not come.

ich war	geblieben (I had stayed)
	hineingegangen (entered)
	eingeschlafen (fallen asleep)
	vorbeigegangen (gone by)
es war	geschehen (it had happened)

The pluperfect and perfect tenses

Look how similar the pluperfect tense is to the perfect tense.

Ich habe Basketball gespielt.   ➡   Ich hatte Basketball gespielt.
I played basketball.   I had played basketball.

Es hat ihm Spaß gemacht.   ➡   Es hatte ihm Spaß gemacht.
It was fun for him.   It had been fun for him.

Wir sind zur Eishalle gegangen.   ➡   Wir waren zur Eishalle gegangen.
We went to the ice rink.   We had gone to the ice rink.

Now try this

Write these sentences in the pluperfect tense.

(a) Ich habe zu Mittag gegessen.
(b) Sie haben als Stadtführer gearbeitet.
(c) Bist du schwimmen gegangen?
(d) Wir sind in Kontakt geblieben.
(e) Sie sind mit dem Rad in die Stadt gefahren.
(f) Ich habe sie vor einigen Monaten besucht, aber damals war sie schon krank.
(g) Bevor ich ins Haus gegangen bin, habe ich ein Gesicht am Fenster gesehen.
(h) Obwohl ich kaum mit ihm gesprochen habe, schien er sehr freundlich zu sein.

Questions

If you opt for the open interaction in the speaking assessment, knowing how to ask questions is an important part of it.

Asking questions

You can swap the pronoun and verb round to form a question:

Du hast einen Hund. You have got a dog.

Hast du einen Hund? Have you got a dog?

Make sure you use a variety of tenses when you ask questions about events at different times.

Sie sind nach Spanien geflogen.
You flew to Spain.

Sind Sie nach Spanien geflogen?
Did you fly to Spain?

Key question words

Wann?	When?
Warum?	Why?
Was?	What?
Wer?	Who?
Wie?	How?
Wo?	Where?

Wohin werden Sie in den Urlaub fahren?
Where will you go on holiday?

Wann sind Sie dorthin gefahren?
When did you go there?

Warum hat Ihnen der Film nicht gefallen?
Why didn't you like the film?

Other question words

Was für ...?	What sort of ...?
Was für Bücher lesen Sie gern?	What sort of books do you like reading?
Wie viele?	How many?
Wie viele Stunden pro Woche treiben Sie Sport?	
How many hours a week do you do sport?	
Wessen?	Whose?
Wessen Idee war das?	Whose idea was that?

Wessen never changes case.

Wen? Wem?	Who(m)?
Wen finden Sie besser?	
Who do you find better?	

Wen is in the accusative case.

Mit wem spielen Sie Squash?
Who do you play squash with?

Wem is in the dative case after mit.

Using welcher (which)

Welcher agrees with the noun it is asking about.

masc	Welcher Sport? Which sport?
fem	Welche Aufgabe? Which activity?
neut	Welches Fach? Which subject?
pl	Welche Fächer? Which lessons?

Welchen Sport finden Sie am einfachsten?
Which sport do you find the easiest?

Welches Fach machst du am liebsten?
Which subject do you like doing best?

Now try this

1 Turn the sentences into questions.
   (a) Sie lesen gern Science-Fiction-Bücher.
   (b) Sie finden Ihre Arbeit anstrengend.
   (c) Sie möchten nur Teilzeit arbeiten.
   (d) Nächsten Sommer werden Sie nach Australien auswandern.

2 Write questions to ask in your speaking assessment.
   (a) Who is your favourite singer?
   (b) When did you last go to the theatre?
   (c) Why did you become a teacher?
   (d) How often do you eat at a restaurant?
   (e) What sort of shops do you particularly like?

Time markers

Here are some ideas to give a flavour of timing to your work – remember to put the verb in SECOND position if you are starting with one of these time markers.

Present tense

aktuell	current(ly)
heute	today
heutzutage	these days
jetzt	now
normalerweise	normally
seit	since / for

Jetzt, wo ich noch Schülerin bin, muss ich viel lernen.
Now, while I am still a pupil, I must work hard.

Past tenses

gestern	yesterday
vorgestern	the day before yesterday
vor drei Monaten	three months ago
letzte Woche	last week
letztes Wochenende	last weekend
früher	previously
als (kleines) Kind	as a (small) child
neulich	recently

Vor sechs Wochen habe ich mir das Bein gebrochen.
I broke my leg six weeks ago.

Future tense

bald	soon
in Zukunft	in future
morgen (früh)	tomorrow (morning)
übermorgen	day after tomorrow
nächste Woche	next week
am nächsten Tag	on the next day

Wenn ich älter bin, werde ich eine gute Stelle finden.
When I am older, I will find a good job.

General

jeden Tag / täglich	every day / daily
wöchentlich	weekly
eines Tages	one day
immer	always
immer noch	still
schon immer	always
am Anfang	at the start
von Zeit zu Zeit	from time to time
sofort	immediately
rechtzeitig	on time
regelmäßig	regularly

Ich habe schon immer in Wales gewohnt.
I have always lived in Wales.

Now try this

Rewrite these sentences with the time expressions provided in brackets.

(a) Ich spiele Klavier. (seit drei Jahren)
(b) Er hat die Hausaufgaben nicht gemacht. (letzte Woche)
(c) Wir werden in den Bergen wandern gehen. (nächsten Sommer)
(d) Wir wollten das Betriebspraktikum nicht machen. (am Anfang)
(e) Man wird alle Lebensmitteln elektronisch kaufen. (in Zukunft)
(f) Ich hoffe, Disneyland zu besuchen. (eines Tages)
(g) Ich hatte Halsschmerzen. (vorgestern)
(h) Sie spielen oft Tennis. (früher)    Watch the tense!

Numbers

Numbers are really important in a variety of contexts so make sure you know them!

Numbers

1 eins	11 elf	21 einundzwanzig	100 hundert
2 zwei	12 zwölf	22 zweiundzwanzig	101 hunderteins
3 drei	13 dreizehn		200 zweihundert
4 vier	14 vierzehn		333 dreihundertdreiunddreißig
5 fünf	15 fünfzehn	all one word –	
6 sechs	16 sechzehn	however long!	
7 sieben	17 siebzehn		no und after dreihundert
8 acht	18 achtzehn	30 dreißig	
9 neun	19 neunzehn	40 vierzig	1000 tausend
10 zehn	20 zwanzig	50 fünfzig	
		60 sechzig	ein Tausend – a thousand
		70 siebzig	eine Million – a million
		80 achtzig	eine Milliarde – a billion
		90 neunzig	eine Billion – a trillion

Ordinal numbers

1st erste	11th elfte	am vierzehnten März	on 14th March
2nd zweite	12th zwölfte	ab dem achten Juni	from 8th June
3rd dritte	13th dreizehnte	vom ersten bis zum	from 1st to 13th
4th vierte	14th vierzehnte	dreizehnten Dezember	December
5th fünfte		nach/vor dem zehnten April	after/before 10th April
6th sechste	20th zwanzigste		
7th siebte	21st einundzwanzigste	seit dem dritten Februar	since 3rd February
8th achte	30th dreißigste		
9th neunte	31st einunddreißigste	YEARS: (im Jahr) neunzehnhundertachtundachtzig	in 1988
10th zehnte		zweitausendzwölf	2012

Now try this LISTENING 67

Listen and complete the number gaps.

(a) [ ]–[ ] . Mai

(b) [:]

(c) € [ ] , [ ]

(d) [ ] . Januar [ ]

(e) € [ ] Millionen

(f) [ ] % Ermäßigung

(g) [:]

(h) [ ] Grad

Vocabulary

These pages cover key German vocabulary that you need to know. This section starts with general terms that are useful in a wide variety of situations and then divides into vocabulary for each of the four main topics covered in this revision guide:

1 High frequency language **2** Personal information **3** Out and about

4 Customer service and transactions **5** Future plans, education and work

F Sections to be learnt by all candidates **H** Sections to be learnt by Higher candidates only

Learning vocabulary is essential preparation for your reading and listening exams. Don't try to learn too much at once – concentrate on learning and testing yourself on a page at a time.

1 High frequency language

Verbs A–E

abfahren	to depart
anfangen	to begin
ankommen	to arrive
annehmen	to accept
anrufen	to phone
antworten	to answer
arbeiten	to work
aufhören	to stop
aufmachen	to open
ausgeben	to spend
ausleihen	to lend
bedienen	to serve
befehlen	to order
begegnen	to meet
beginnen	to begin
begleiten	to accompany
bekommen	to receive
benutzen	to use
beraten	to advise
beschließen	to decide
beschreiben	to describe
besprechen	to discuss
bestellen	to order
besuchen	to visit
bevorzugen	to prefer
bleiben	to stay
brauchen	to need
bringen	to bring
danken	to thank
dauern	to last
denken	to think
drücken	to push
eilen	to hurry
einkaufen	to shop
einladen	to invite
einschalten	to turn on
einschlafen	to fall asleep
eintreten	to enter
empfehlen	to recommend

Verbs E–K

enden	to finish, end
erklären	to explain
erlauben	to allow
erreichen	to reach
erzählen	to tell
fallen	to fall
fallen lassen	to drop
fehlen	to miss
fernsehen	to watch TV
finden	to find
fliehen	to escape
folgen	to follow
fragen	to ask
fühlen	to feel
führen	to lead
füllen	to fill
geben	to give
gefallen	to please
gehören	to belong
gelingen	to succeed
geschehen	to happen
gewinnen	to win
glauben	to think, believe
haben	to have
halten	to stop, hold
hassen	to hate
heißen	to be called
helfen	to help
hineingehen	to enter
hoffen	to hope
holen	to fetch
hören	to hear
kaufen	to buy
kennen	to know
kleben	to stick
klettern	to climb
klingeln	to ring
klopfen	to knock
kommen	to come
kosten	to cost

Verbs L–S

lächeln	to smile
lachen	to laugh
lassen	to leave
laufen	to walk, run
leben	to live
legen	to lay
leihen	to borrow, hire
lesen	to read
lieben	to love
liegen	to lie
lügen	to tell a lie
meinen	to think, say
mieten	to rent
mitteilen	to inform
nachsehen	to check
nehmen	to take
nennen	to call
notieren	to note
öffnen	to open
organisieren	to organise
passieren	to happen
planen	to plan
plaudern	to chat
raten	to advise
rechnen	to count
reden	to talk
reparieren	to repair
retten	to save
sagen	to say
schauen	to look
scheinen	to seem, shine
schenken	to give (gift)
schicken	to send
schlagen	to knock, hit
schließen	to shut
schreiben	to write
sehen	to see
sich ärgern	to get angry
sich beeilen	to hurry
sich befinden	to be located

Now try this

Pick five verbs at random from each column and see if you can write each one in the present, perfect and future tense for the **ich** form. Check your answers by looking at pages 97–105.

① High frequency language

Verbs S–Z

sich entscheiden	to decide
sich erinnern an	to remember
sich freuen auf	to look forward to
sich langweilen	to get bored
sich streiten	to argue
sitzen	to sit
spazieren	to walk
sprechen	to speak
springen	to jump
stecken	to place
stehlen	to steal
steigen	to climb, get on
stellen	to put
stoppen	to stop
streiten	to argue
studieren	to study
tippen	to type
tragen	to wear, carry
treffen	to meet
trinken	to drink
unterschreiben	to sign
verbessern	to improve
verbringen	to spend (time)
verdienen	to earn
vergeben	to forgive
vergessen	to forget
verhindern	to prevent
verkaufen	to sell
verlassen	to leave
verlieren	to lose
vermeiden	to avoid
versprechen	to promise
verstehen	to understand
versuchen	to try
verzeihen	to forgive
vorbeigehen	to pass by
vorhaben	to intend
vorstellen	to introduce
wählen	to choose, dial
warten auf	to wait for
wechseln	to change
werden	to become
wiederholen	to repeat
wissen	to know
wohnen	to live
wünschen	to wish
zahlen	to pay
zählen	to count
zeigen	to show
zuhören	to listen
zumachen	to close

fahren to drive

schlafen to sleep

gehen to walk, go

weinen to cry

essen to eat

werfen to throw

zurückfahren	to return (by car)
zurückgehen	to return (on foot)
zurückkommen	to come back
zurückstellen	to put back
zusehen	to watch

Modal verbs

dürfen	to be allowed to
können	to be able to
mögen	to like
müssen	to have to
sollen	to be supposed to
wollen	to want

Adverbs

besonders	especially
da	there
da drüben	over there
dort	there
fast	almost
gern	willingly
hier	here
immer	always, still

irgendwo	somewhere
jedoch	however
leider	unfortunately
lieber	rather
manchmal	sometimes
mehr	more
mitten	in the middle of
neulich	recently
nie	never
oben	above, upstairs
oft	often
regelmäßig	regularly
rückwärts	backwards
schnell	quickly
schon	already
sehr	very
sofort	immediately
unten	below
unterwegs	en route
vielleicht	perhaps
vorwärts	forwards
wahrscheinlich	probably
wirklich	really
ziemlich	rather / quite
zu	too

Now try this

Choose 20 verbs you didn't know from this page and the previous one and write them in German.
Close the book and try to write the English next to each one. Check back, then test yourself again on any you didn't get right.

① High frequency language

Adjectives A–F

aktuell	current
all-	all
allein	alone
allgemein	general
anders-	other
ärgerlich	annoying
artig	well behaved
aufregend	exciting
ausgezeichnet	excellent
bequem	comfortable
bereit	ready
beschäftigt	busy
bestimmt	definite
böse	angry
breit	broad
dankbar	grateful
dicht	dense
draußen	outside
dreckig	dirty
drinnen	inside
dumm	stupid
dynamisch	dynamic
echt	real
ehemalig	old, former
eigen	own
eilig	in a hurry
einzig	only
ekelhaft	disgusting
eng	narrow
ermüdend	tiring
ernst	serious
erschöpft	exhausted
erst	first
erstaunt	astonished
falsch	false
fantastisch	great
faul	lazy
fertig	ready
fleißig	hard-working
flexibel	flexible
frei	free

Adjectives G–N

gebrochen	broken
gefährlich	dangerous
genau	exact
geöffnet	open
geschlossen	closed
gesund	healthy
gleich	similar, same
glücklich	happy
goldig	charming
großartig	magnificent
gültig	valid
gut	good
gut gelaunt	in a good mood
hart	severe, unkind
häßlich	ugly
heiß	hot
hoch	high
hübsch	pretty
jünger	younger
kaputt	broken
klar	clear
klasse	sensational
komisch	funny
kostenlos	free (cost)
krank	ill
kurz	short
lang	long
langweilig	boring
launisch	moody
laut	noisy
lautlos	silent
leer	empty
leicht	easy
leise	quiet
letzte	last
Lieblings-	favourite
lustig	funny
müde	tired
nächst-	next
nah	near
nett	kind, nice
neu	new

Farbe (f)	colour
hell	light
dunkel	dark
blau	
braun	
gelb	
grau	
grün	
lila	
rosa	
rot	
schwarz	
weiß	

Adjectives N–R

niedrig	low
nötig	necessary
notwendig	necessary
nützlich	useful
offen	open
perfekt	perfect
prima	great, marvellous
reich	rich
reif	mature, ripe
richtig	true, right
ruhig	peaceful, calm
rund	round

jung   alt

dick   dünn

groß   klein

Now try this

Look around the room you are in. Try to use 10 German adjectives to describe the room or the objects in it. Then think of a friend you have seen today. Try to use 10 German adjectives to describe their appearance, their personality and their clothing.

113

① High frequency language

Adjectives S–Z

satt	full
sauber	clean
schlecht	bad
schmal	narrow
schmutzig	dirty
schnell	fast, quick
schön	beautiful
schrecklich	awful, terrible
schüchtern	shy
schwach	weak
schwer	heavy, difficult
schwierig	difficult
spannend	exciting
stark	strong
steil	steep
stolz	proud
streng	strict
teuer	expensive
toll	great
traurig	sad
typisch	typical
überrascht	surprised
umweltfeindlich	eco-unfriendly
umweltfreundlich	eco-friendly
unglaublich	unbelievable
unterschiedlich	variable
unvorstellbar	unimaginable
verantwortlich	responsible
voll	full
wahr	true
weich	soft
weit	far
wertvoll	valuable
wichtig	important
wirklich	real
wunderbar	marvellous
zahlreich	numerous
zornig	angry
zufrieden	pleased, satisfied
zusammen	together

Connecting words

aber	but
also	so
auch	also, too
außerdem	moreover
dafür	from that
dann	then
deshalb	for this reason
dewegen	for this reason
nachher	afterwards
oder	or
übrigens	moreover
und	and
vorher	beforehand
zuerst	first of all

Quantities

ein bisschen	a little of
ein Drittel	a third of
ein Dutzend	a dozen
ein Glas	a jar of
ein Stück	a piece of
eine Dose	a tin, box of
eine Flasche	a bottle of
eine Packung	a packet of
eine Scheibe	a slice of
eine Tafel	a bar of
eine Tüte	a bag of
genug	enough
mehrere	several
viele	many

Time expressions

ab	from
ab und zu	from time to time
Abend (m)	evening
am Anfang	at the start
bald	soon
früh	early
gestern	yesterday
heute	today
heutzutage	nowadays
immer	always
immer noch	still
jetzt	now
meistens	mostly
Minute (f)	minute
Mittag (m)	midday
Mitternacht (f)	midnight
morgen	tomorrow
Morgen (m)	morning
morgen früh	tomorrow a.m.
Nachmittag (m)	afternoon
nächst-	next
Nacht (f)	night
pünktlich	on time
rechtzeitig	on time
seit	since
sofort	immediately
spät	late
später	later
Tag (m)	day
täglich	every day
übermorgen	day after tomorrow
von Zeit zu Zeit	from time to time
Vormittag (m)	morning
Woche (f)	week
Wochenende (n)	weekend
wöchentlich	weekly

ein kleines
Stück Kuchen

ein großes
Stück Kuchen

ein Glas
Marmelade

eine Tafel
Schokolade

eine Packung
Chips

eine Flasche
Medizin

eine Scheibe
Toast

eine Dose
Erbsen

Now try this

Test yourself on the time expressions above by covering up the English column and then writing down the English translations yourself. Compare your answers with the list above. How many have you got right?

1 High frequency language

Questions

wann?	when?
warum?	why?
was?	what?
was für?	what sort of?
wen? wem?	whom?
wer?	who?
wessen?	whose?
wie?	how?
wie viel(e)?	how much / many?
wo?	where?

Other high frequency words

alle	everyone
Art (f)	type
das	that
Ding (n)	thing
Ende (n)	end
Form (f)	shape
Frau (f)	Mrs
Gegenstand (m)	object
Herr (m)	Mr
irgendetwas	something
ja	yes
jeder	everybody
jemand	someone
Mal (n)	time
Mitte (f)	middle
nein	no
Nummer (f)	number
ob	whether
Sache (f)	thing
weil	because
Weise (f)	way
wenn	if
wie	as, like
Zahl (f)	figure
zum Beispiel	for example

	Montag Monday	Dienstag Tuesday	Mittwoch Wednesday	Donnerstag Thursday	Freitag Friday	Samstag / Sonnabend Saturday	Sonntag Sunday
07.00							
08.00							
09.00							
10.00							
11.00							
12.00							
13.00							
14.00							
15.00							
16.00							
17.00							
18.00							

Social conventions

alles Gute	all the best	danke schön	thank you
auf Wiedersehen	goodbye	Entschuldigung	excuse me
bis bald	see you soon	Grüß Gott	hello
bis Morgen	see you tomorrow	gute Nacht	goodnight
		guten Abend	good evening
bis später	see you later	guten Tag	hello, good day
bitte	please		
bitte schön	you're welcome	mit bestem Gruß	best wishes
		wie bitte?	pardon?

Months

Januar · Februar · März · April · Mai · Juni

Juli · August · September · Oktober · November · Dezember

Now try this

Practise the days of the week and the months of the year by translating the birthdays of family and friends into German.

① High frequency language

Prepositions

an	at
auf	on
aus	out of
außer	except
bei	with, at (house)
bis	until
durch	through
entlang	along
für	for
gegen	towards
gegenüber	opposite
hinter	behind
in	in, into
mit	with
nach	after
neben	next to
ohne	without
seit	since
statt	instead of
trotz	despite
über	above, over
um	around
unter	beneath, under
von	from
vor	in front of
während	during
wegen	because of
zu	to
zwischen	between

Continents

Afrika	Africa
Asien	Asia
Australien	Australia
Europa	Europe
Nordamerika	North America
Südamerika	South America

Countries

Belgien	Belgium
Dänemark	Denmark
die Niederlande	Netherlands
Griechenland	Greece
Indien	India
Russland	Russia
Deutschland	
die Schweiz	
die Türkei	
die Vereinigten Staaten	
England	
Frankreich	
Großbritannien	
Irland	
Italien	
Österreich	
Schottland	
Spanien	
Wales	

Nationalities

Note that the first line of each entry in this section is the noun (a German man / woman, etc.). The second line is the adjective.

Afrikaner/in afrikanisch	African
Amerikaner/in amerikanisch	American
Belgier/in belgisch	Belgian
Brite/Britin britisch	British
Däne/Dänin dänisch	Danish
Deutsche(r) deutsch	German
Engländer/in englisch	English
Europäer/in europäisch	European
Franzose/Französin französisch	French
Grieche/Griechin griechisch	Greek
Ire/Irin, irisch	Irish
Italiener/in italienisch	Italian
Niederländer/in niederländisch	Dutch
Österreicher/in österreichisch	Austrian
Russe/Russin russisch	Russian
Schotte/Schottin schottisch	Scottish
Schweizer/in schweizerisch	Swiss
Spanier/in spanisch	Spanish
Waliser/in walisisch	Welsh

Now try this

Match the German place names to their English equivalents.

(a)	Bayern	1	Vienna
(b)	der Ärmelkanal	2	Bavaria
(c)	der Bodensee	3	Geneva
(d)	der Schwarzwald	4	Danube
(e)	die Alpen	5	Black Forest
(f)	die Donau	6	Cologne
(g)	Genf	7	English Channel
(h)	Köln	8	Lake Constance
(i)	München	9	Munich
(j)	Wien	10	Alps

(Answers are on page 133.)

② Personal information

General interests

Ich spiele ...
I play ...

Geige   Trompete   Flöte   Schlagzeug

Klarinette   Klavier   Blockflöte

Abenteuerfilm	adventure film
altmodisch	old-fashioned
Anfang (m)	beginning
anziehen	to put on
aufregend	exciting
Ausrüstung (f)	equipment
Buch (n)	book
Comicheft (n)	comic
fernsehen	to watch TV
Fernseher (m)	TV set
gratis	free (of charge)
Gruppe (f)	group
Handy (n)	mobile phone
Kenntnis (f)	knowledge
klassisch	classical
kochen	to cook
Krimi (m)	thriller
lehrreich	informative
Lesen (n)	reading
Liebesfilm (m)	romantic film
Lieblings-	favourite
Lied (n)	song
Lust haben	to want to
machen	to do, make
mitkommen	to accompany
modisch	fashionable
Nachrichten (pl)	news
Nachteil (m)	disadvantage
Quizsendung (f)	quiz show
Radfahren (n)	cycling
rennen	to run
sammeln	to collect
Sänger (m)	singer
schick	chic, smart
Seifenoper (f)	soap opera
Sendung (f)	TV programme
Serie (f)	series
sich amüsieren	to enjoy
sich schminken	to put on make-up
sich unterhalten	to chat
simsen	to text
sparsam	thrifty
Spaß (m)	fun
spazieren gehen	to take a walk
Spiel (n)	game
Spieler (m)	player
Spielzeug (n)	toy
Stereoanlage (f)	stereo system
synchronisiert	dubbed (film)
Tagesschau (f)	news
Taschengeld (n)	pocket money

Tätowierung (f)	tattoo
Technologie (f)	technology
Umwelt (f)	environment
umweltfeindlich	eco-unfriendly
umweltfreundlich	eco-friendly
Unterhaltung (f)	entertainment
vorschlagen	to suggest
Vorteil (m)	advantage
Zeichentrickfilm (m)	cartoon
Zeitschrift (f)	magazine
Zeitung (f)	newspaper
zu Hause	at home
Zuschauer (m)	viewer

aufnehmen	to record
begleiten	to accompany
Fernbedienung (f)	remote control
gelangweilt	bored
Gruselfilm (m)	horror film
gruselig	creepy
plaudern	to chat, natter
Rennen (n)	race, racing
spannend	exciting
Überraschung (f)	surprise
umsonst	free of charge
Untertitel (f)	subtitle
Vergnügen (n)	pleasure
vorziehen	to prefer
Wettbewerb (m)	competition

Leisure activities

Aktivität (f)	activity
anbieten	to offer
Angebot (n)	offer
angeln	to fish
Ausflug (m)	excursion
ausgehen	to go out
Bühne (f)	stage
bummeln	to go for a stroll
Computerspiel (n)	computer game
eislaufen	to ice skate
faulenzen	to laze about

Freibad (n)	open air pool
Freizeit (f)	leisure
Fußball	football
Grill (m)	barbecue
Jugendklub (m)	youth club
kegeln	to bowl
Kino (n)	cinema
Leichtathletik (f)	athletics
Mannschaft (f)	team
Meisterschaft (f)	championship
mitgehen	to go along
Mitglied (n)	member
Pferd (n)	horse
Radfahren (n)	cycling
reiten	to ride (horse)
Rollschuh laufen	to roller skate
Schach (n)	chess
schießen	to shoot
Schlittschuhlaufen	ice skating
schwimmen	to swim
Segelboot (n)	sailing boat
segeln	to sail
sich treffen mit	to meet with
Skifahren (n)	skiing
Spaziergang (m)	walk
Sport treiben	to do sport
Sportausrüstung	sports kit
Sportplatz (m)	sports ground
tanzen	to dance
Theaterstück (n)	play (theatre)
Tischtennis (n)	table tennis
Tor (n)	goal (football)
turnen	to exercise, do gymnastics
Verein (m)	club
Vorstellung (f)	performance
wandern	to hike, ramble
Wasserski (n)	water skiing

Angelrute (f)	fishing rod
annehmen	to accept
Bergsteigen (n)	mountaineering
Bogenschießen (n)	archery
Klettern (n)	(rock) climbing
Schauspiel (n)	play (theatre)
sich ausruhen	to rest, relax
Sportart (f)	sport
tauchen	to dive

Now try this

To help you learn the leisure activities vocabulary, make a list of five activities that you like doing and five activities that you don't like doing and then memorise them.

② Personal information

Friends and family

(nicht) leiden	to (dis)like
allein	alone
alt	old
älter	older
Alter (n)	age
altmodisch	old-fashioned
arm	poor
auf die Nerven gehen	to annoy
Augen (pl)	eyes
auskommen mit	to get on with
Ausländer (f)	foreigner
ausländisch	foreign
aussehen	to look
babysitten	to babysit
Badezimmer (n)	bathroom
Bart (m)	beard
berühmt	famous
Besuch (m)	visit
besuchen	to visit
bevorzugen	to prefer
Bild (n)	picture
blöd	foolish, silly
Blödsinn (m)	nonsense
böse	angry, cross
Brieffreund (m)	penfriend
Brille (f)	glasses
Bruder (m)	brother
Cousin/e (m/f)	cousin
Doppelhaus (n)	semi-detached house
egoistisch	selfish
Ehe (f)	marriage
ehrlich	honest
Einfamilienhaus (n)	detached house
einladen	to invite
Einladung (f)	invitation
einsam	lonely
einverstanden	agreed
Einzelkind (n)	only child
Eltern (pl)	parents
Enkelkind (n)	grandchild
ernst	serious
Erwachsene (m/f)	adult
Familie (f)	family
Feier (f)	party
feiern	to celebrate
Frau (f)	wife, woman
frech	cheeky

Freund (m)	male friend
Freundin (f)	female friend
freundlich	friendly
Freundschaft (f)	friendship
geboren	born
Geburt (f)	birth
Geburtsdatum (n)	date of birth
Geburtsort (m)	birthplace
Geburtstag (m)	birthday
geduldig	patient
Gefühl (n)	feeling
gemein	mean, nasty
gern haben	to like
Geschenk (n)	present
geschieden	divorced
Geschwister (pl)	siblings
Gesicht (n)	face
getrennt	separated
glatt	straight (hair)
gratulieren	to congratulate
großartig	magnificent
Großeltern (pl)	grandparents
Großmutter (f)	grandmother
Großvater (m)	grandfather
gut / schlecht gelaunt	in a good / bad mood
Haar (n)	hair
Halb-	half-
hässlich	ugly
Haus (n)	house
Haushalt (m)	household
Haustier (n)	pet
Hautfarbe (f)	skin colour
Heim (n)	home
heiraten	to get married
heißen	to be called
hilfsbereit	helpful
Hochzeit (f)	wedding
höflich	polite
hübsch	pretty
humorvoll	humorous
Hund (m)	dog
Jahr (n)	year
Jugendliche (m/f)	young person
jung	young
Junge (m)	boy
Katze (f)	cat
kennen	to know
Kind (n)	child
Kinn (n)	chin
komisch	funny
kritisieren	to criticise
Kuss (m)	kiss
küssen	to kiss
Laune (f)	mood
Leben (n)	life

lebhaft	lively
ledig	unmarried
Leute (pl)	people
Licht (n)	light
lieb	likeable
lockig	curly
lustig	funny
Mädchen (n)	girl
Mund (m)	mouth
Mutter (f)	mother
Nachbar (m)	neighbour
Nase (f)	nose
nett	nice, kind
Ohr (n)	ear
Ohrringe (pl)	earrings
Oma (f)	grandma
Onkel (m)	uncle
Opa (m)	grandad
ordentlich	tidy
Persönlichkeit (f)	personality
pessimistisch	pessimistic
Postleitzahl (f)	postcode
reich	rich
Reihenhaus (n)	terrace house
sauer	sour, cross
schlank	thin
Schnurrbart (m)	moustache
schön	beautiful
schüchtern	shy
schwätzen	to chat
Schwester (f)	sister
Schwiegersohn (m) /-tochter (f)	son / daughter-in-law
selbst	self
sich freuen auf	to look forward
sich kümmern um	to look after
sich streiten	to argue
sich trennen	to separate
sich verloben	to get engaged
sich verstehen	to get on
sich vorstellen	to introduce
Sohn (m)	son
sorgen für	to care for
spenden	to donate
Spitzname (m)	nickname
Stief-	step-
still	quiet
Streit (m)	argument
sympathisch	nice, likeable
Tante (f)	aunt
Taufe (f)	christening
Tochter (f)	daughter
tot	dead
Traum (m)	dream
traurig	sad
Trauring (m)	wedding ring
Typ (m)	guy, bloke

Now try this

To help you learn the personality adjectives, write out the German words in three lists: positive, negative and neutral. Then memorise five adjectives that could describe you.

② Personal information

Umfrage (f)	survey
unternehmungs-lustig	adventurous
unterstützen	to support
Vater (m)	father
verheiratet	married
verliebt	in love
verlobt	engaged
Vorname (m)	first name
witzig	funny, witty
Wohnort (m)	home location
Wohnung (f)	flat
zufrieden	satisfied
Zuhause (n)	home
Zwillinge (pl)	twins

ähnlich	similar
alleinstehend	single
angeberisch	pretentious
Anschrift (f)	address
auf Grund	based on
ausgeglichen	well-balanced
bedürftig	needy, in need
Begegnung (f)	meeting
Bekannte (m/f)	acquaintance
benachteiligen	to disadvantage
Beziehung (f)	relationship
Braut (f)	bride
Bräutigam (m)	bridegroom
eifersüchtig	jealous
eine gute Tat	a good deed
eingebildet	conceited
Enkel (m)	grandson
erleben	to experience
Geschlecht (n)	gender, sex
Glatze (f)	bald head
großzügig	generous
leiden	to suffer
minderjährig	underage
Neffe (m)	nephew
Nichte (f)	niece
obdachlos	homeless
Pickel (m)	pimple
Rentner (m)	pensioner
schikanieren	to pick on
selbständig	independent
selbstbewusst	self-confident
treu	loyal, faithful
verrückt	mad, crazy
Verwandte (m/f)	relation
volljährig	of age (18+)
Vorbild (n)	role model
zuverlässig	reliable

Lifestyle: healthy living and exercise

abnehmen	to lose weight
Alkohol (m)	alcohol
alkoholisch	alcoholic
alt	old
Alter (n)	age
Angst haben	to be afraid
Arm (m)	arm
atmen	to breathe
aufgeben	to give up
aufhören	to stop
Bauch (m)	stomach
Bein (n)	leg
betrunken	drunk
brechen	to break
Diät machen	to diet
dick	fat
Droge (f)	drug
dünn	thin
Durchfall (m)	diarrhoea
Durst (m)	thirst
durstig	thirsty
Erkältung (f)	cold
erste Hilfe	first aid
fettig	fatty, greasy
Fieber (n)	temperature
Finger (m)	finger
Fuß (m)	foot
gebrochen	broken
gesund	healthy
Gesundheit (f)	health
glücklich	happy
Grippe (f)	flu
Hals (m)	neck, throat
Hand (f)	hand
Herz (n)	heart
husten	to cough
Knie (n)	knee
Kopf (m)	head
Körper (m)	body
köstlich	delicious
laufen	to run
lebendig	lively
Leber (f)	liver
Lunge (f)	lung
Magen (m)	stomach
mager	low-fat
Medikament (n)	medicine
nervös	nervous
rauchen	to smoke
Raucher (m)	smoker
riechen	to smell
Rücken (m)	back (body)
Ruhe (f)	calm, peace

schlimm	bad
schmecken	to taste
Schmerz (m)	pain
Schulter (f)	shoulder
sich entspannen	to relax
sich fit halten	to keep fit
sich fühlen	to feel
sich verletzen	to harm, injure
sportlich	sporty
Spritze (f)	injection
spritzen	to inject
sterben	to die
stressig	stressful
übel	sick, ill
Unfall (m)	accident
ungesund	unhealthy
Vegetarier (m)	vegetarian
Verletzung (f)	injury
Verstopfung (f)	constipation
vorbereiten	to prepare
weh tun	to hurt
Zahn (m)	tooth
Zigarette (f)	cigarette
zunehmen	to put on weight

abhängig	addicted
Ballaststoff (m)	dietary fibre
Behandlung (f)	treatment
bewusstlos	unconscious
Biokost (f)	organic food
Blut (n)	blood
Entziehungskur (f)	rehab
ermüdend	tiring
fettarm	low fat
Fettleibigkeit (f)	obesity
Fußgelenk (n)	ankle
Gehirn (n)	brain
Geruch (m)	smell
Geschmack (m)	taste
Heuschnupfen (m)	hay fever
Krebs (m)	cancer
magersüchtig	anorexic
Mehl (n)	flour
Nahrung (f)	food
Nuss (f)	nut
Rauschgift (n)	drug(s)
Schnupfen (m)	cold
schwindlig	dizzy
sich erholen	to recover
sich gewöhnen an	to get used to
sich trimmen	to keep fit
Sucht (f)	addiction
süchtig	addicted
übergewichtig	overweight
verstauchen	to sprain

Now try this

Write at least 10 body parts on German from memory. Look at the page and check you spelling.

③ Out and about

Visitor information

Ausflug (m)	outing
Ausgang (m)	exit
Auskunft (f)	information
Ausstellung (f)	exhibition
Autobahn (f)	motorway
Autovermietung (f)	car hire
Berg (m)	mountain
Burg (f)	castle
Bürgersteig (m)	pavement
Büro (n)	office
Dom (m)	cathedral
Dorf (n)	village
draußen	outside
Eingang (m)	entrance
Eintrittsgeld (n)	admission
Einwohner (m)	inhabitant
Ermäßigung (f)	reduction
Fahrradverleih (m)	bike hire
Feiertag (m)	public holiday
Feld (n)	field
Fest (n)	festival
flach	flat
Freizeitpark (m)	theme park
Fußgänger (m)	pedestrian
Gegend (f)	area
geöffnet	open
geschlossen	closed
Hauptstadt (f)	capital city
Hotelverzeichnis (n)	hotel list
Hügel (m)	hill
im Ausland	abroad
im Freien	in the open air
im Frühling	in spring
im Herbst	in autumn
im Sommer	in summer
im Winter	in winter
Insel (f)	island
Küste (f)	coast
Land (n)	country
Landschaft (f)	countryside
Luftverschmutzung (f)	air pollution
malerisch	picturesque
Marktplatz (m)	market square
Meer (n)	sea
Müll (m)	rubbish
Nachtleben (n)	nightlife
Öffnungszeiten (pl)	opening hours

Ort (m)	place
Preisliste (f)	price list
Prospekt (m)	leaflet
ruhig	quiet
Rundfahrt (f)	tour
Rundgang (m)	tour (walking)
Schild (n)	sign
Schloss (n)	castle
See (f)	sea
See (m)	lake
sehenswert	worth seeing
Sehenswürdigkeiten (pl)	sights
Stadt (f)	town
Stadtplan (m)	town map
Stadtrand (m)	outskirts
Stadtteil (m)	part of town
Stadtviertel (n)	district
Stadtzentrum (n)	town centre
Strand (m)	beach
Straßenkarte (f)	road map
Termin (m)	appointment
Turm (m)	tower
verboten	forbidden
Verkehrsamt (n)	tourist office
Verschmutzung (f)	pollution
Vorort (m)	suburb
Vorstellung (f)	performance
Wald (m)	wood, forest

Andenken (n)	souvenir
Aufenthalt (m)	stay
Bodensee (m)	Lake Constance
Brunnen (m)	fountain
Erinnerung (f)	memory
Erlebnis (n)	experience
Feuerwerk (n)	firework
Flohmarkt (m)	flea market
Gastfreundschaft (f)	hospitality
Gebiet (n)	area
Gebirge (m)	mountains
Genf	Geneva
Grünanlage (f)	park
Klimaanlage (f)	air conditioning
Notausgang (m)	emergency exit
stattfinden	to take place
Tiergarten (m)	zoo
Umgebung (f)	surrounding area
Umzug (m)	procession
Veranstaltung (f)	event
Zoll (m)	customs

Weather

bedeckt	overcast
bewölkt	cloudy
es donnert	it's thundering
es friert	it's freezing
frostig	frosty
heiß	hot
heiter	bright
kalt	cold
nass	wet
neblig	foggy
regnerisch	rainy
schlecht	bad
sonnig	sunny
trocken	dry
wolkig	cloudy
Gewitter (n)	thunder storm
Grad (m)	degree
Himmel (m)	sky
Hitze (f)	heat
Jahreszeit (f)	season
Klima (n)	climate
Regen (m)	rain
Schnee (m)	snow
Sturm (m)	storm
Wolke (f)	cloud

die Sonne scheint   es blitzt

es ist windig   es regnet

es schneit

Aufheiterung (f)	bright spell
aufklären	to brighten up
Durchschnittstemperatur (f)	average temperature
hageln	to hail
Niederschlag (m)	rainfall
niedrig	low
stürmisch	stormy
wechselhaft	changeable

Now try this

Test this vocabulary, and your knowledge of tenses, by trying to describe the weather yesterday, the weather today, and what you hope the weather will be like tomorrow.

③ Out and about

Local amenities

das Stadion

der Dom

der Flughafen

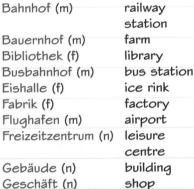
der Bahnhof

die Post

Abfalleimer (m)	rubbish bin
Bahnhof (m)	railway station
Bauernhof (m)	farm
Bibliothek (f)	library
Busbahnhof (m)	bus station
Eishalle (f)	ice rink
Fabrik (f)	factory
Flughafen (m)	airport
Freizeitzentrum (n)	leisure centre
Gebäude (n)	building
Geschäft (n)	shop
Hafen (m)	port
Hallenbad (n)	indoor pool
Hochhaus (n)	tower block
Kino (n)	cinema
Kirche (f)	church
Kneipe (f)	pub
Kunstgalerie (f)	art gallery
Laden (m)	shop
Palast (m)	palace
Platz (m)	square
Rathaus (n)	town hall
Schnellimbiss (m)	snack bar
Schwimmbad (n)	swimming pool
Sparkasse (f)	savings bank
Spielplatz (m)	playground
Sportzentrum (n)	sports centre
Tankstelle (f)	petrol station
Wäscherei (f)	laundry
Waschsalon (m)	launderette
Zeitungskiosk (m)	paper stall

Geldautomat (m)	cashpoint
Postamt (n)	post office

Deutschland

im Norden
im Westen
im Osten
im Süden

Accommodation

ankommen	to arrive
Ankunft (f)	arrival
Aufzug (m)	lift
Ausgang (m)	exit
Aussicht (f)	view
Badetuch (n)	towel
Badewanne (f)	bath tub
Badezimmer (n)	bathroom
Balkon (m)	balcony
besetzt	occupied
Betttuch (n)	sheet
Bettwäsche (f)	bedlinen
Boden (m)	floor
Campingplatz (m)	campsite
Doppelzimmer (n)	double room
Dorf (n)	village
Dusche (f)	shower
Einzelzimmer (n)	single room
Empfang (m)	reception
Erdgeschoss (n)	ground floor
Essecke (f)	dining area
Esszimmer (n)	dining room
Etage (f)	floor (1st, 2nd)
Etagenbett (n)	bunk bed
Fahrstuhl (m)	lift
Fenster (n)	window
Fernsehapparat (n)	TV set
frei	free, available

funktionieren	to work
Gepäck (n)	luggage
Halbpension (f)	half board
Haustür (f)	(front) door
Heizung (f)	heating
im ersten Stock	on first floor
im Voraus	in advance
inbegriffen	included
Jugendherberge (f)	youth hostel
Kleiderschrank (m)	wardrobe
Koffer (m)	suitcase
Kopfkissen (n)	pillow
Küche (f)	kitchen
Mehrbettzimmer	shared room
Miete (f)	rent
mieten	to rent
mit Blick auf	with a view of
möbliert	furnished
Pension (f)	B&B
Schlafsack (m)	sleeping bag
Schlafzimmer (n)	bedroom
Schlüssel (m)	key
Seife (f)	soap
Stock (m)	floor (1st, 2nd)
Treppe (f)	staircase
Trinkwasser (n)	drinking water
übernachten	to stay the night
Übernachtung (f)	overnight stay
Untergeschoss (n)	basement
Unterkunft (f)	accommodation

Now try this

Without looking at the book, think about all of the amenities in your local town or city and make a list of them in German. Open the book and then check your spelling.

❸ Out and about

Vollpension (f)	full board
Vorhang (m)	curtain
Waschbecken (n)	wash basin
Wohnwagen (m)	caravan
Wohnzimmer (n)	sitting room
Zahnbürste (f)	toothbrush
Zahnpasta (f)	toothpaste
Zelt (n)	tent
zelten	to camp (tent)
Zweibettzimmer (n)	twin room

Anmeldung (f)	registration
Aufenthalt (m)	stay
ausschalten	to switch off
bestätigen	to confirm
einschalten	to switch on
Hausordnung (f)	house rules
Mietwohnung (f)	rented flat
unterbringen	to accommodate
Unterkunft und Verpflegung	board and lodgings

Transport

FOUNDATION F

Abgase (pl)	exhaust fumes
Abfahrt (f)	departure
Abflug (m)	plane departure
Abteil (n)	compartment
Ankunft (f)	arrival
Anschluss (m)	connection
Ausfahrt (f)	exit (vehicles)

aussteigen	to get off
Bahn (f)	railway
Bahnsteig (m)	platform
Benzin (n)	petrol
besetzt	occupied (seat)
bleifrei	unleaded
Dampfer (m)	steamer
einfach	single (ticket)
Einfahrt (f)	entrance (road)
einsteigen	to get on (train)
Einzelfahrkarte (f)	single ticket
entwerten	to validate ticket
Fähre (f)	ferry
Fahrkarte (f)	ticket
Fahrplan (m)	timetable
Fahrt (f)	journey, trip
Führerschein (m)	driving licence
Gepäckaufbewahrung (f)	left luggage
Gleis (n)	platform
Haltestelle (f)	stop (bus, train)
hin und zurück	return (ticket)
Karte (f)	ticket
Motor (m)	engine
öffentliche Verkehrsmittel	public transport
Panne (f)	breakdown
Platz (m)	seat
Reise (f)	journey
Rückfahrkarte (f)	return ticket
S-Bahn (f)	suburban train
schaden	to harm
schädlich	harmful
Schalter (m)	counter
Schlafwagen (m)	sleeper

Schließfach (n)	luggage locker
sich verspäten	to be late
Speisewagen (m)	dining car
Stau (m)	traffic jam
tanken	to fill with petrol
U-Bahn (f)	underground
Überfahrt (f)	crossing
Umleitung (f)	diversion
umsteigen	to change
Verbindung (f)	connection
Verkehr (m)	traffic
Verkehrsunfall (m)	traffic accident
verpassen	to miss
verschmutzen	to pollute
Verspätung (f)	delay
Vorfahrt (f)	priority
Wagen (m)	car, carriage
Wand (f)	wall (inside)
Wartesaal (m)	waiting room
Zuschlag (m)	supplement

HIGHER H

bremsen	to brake
Eilzug (m)	fast train
Fahrzeug (n)	vehicle
Geschwindigkeit (f)	speed
Hubschrauber (m)	helicopter
Lärm (m)	noise
Rastplatz (m)	picnic area
Raststätte (f)	motorway services
sich beeilen	to hurry
Stoßzeit (f)	rush hour
überholen	to overtake

Auto (n)

Zug (m)

Boot (n)

Bus (m)

Fahrrad (n)

Flugzeug (n)

Lastwagen (m)

Mofa (n)

Motorrad (n)

Straßenbahn (f)

Now try this

Make a list of all the forms of transport you have used in the past year. Memorise the words then test yourself on the German spellings.

④ Customer service and transactions

Directions

Ampel (f)	traffic lights
Brücke (f)	bridge
Ecke (f)	corner
Einbahnstraße (f)	one-way street
Fluß (m)	river
geradeaus	straight on
Kreisverkehr (m)	roundabout
Kreuzung (f)	crossroads
Landkarte (f)	map
Richtung (f)	direction
sich befinden	to be situated
überqueren	to cross
weit	far
zu Fuß	on foot

	auf der linken Seite
	on the left

	auf der rechten Seite
	on the right

	links
	left

	rechts
	right

	geradeaus
	straight on

Fußgänger-überweg (m)	pedestrian crossing

Cafés / restaurants

Abendessen (n)	evening meal
alkoholfrei	non-alcoholic
Apfelsine (f)	orange
Aprikose (f)	apricot
Aufschnitt (m)	cold sliced meat
Bargeld (n)	cash
bedienen	to serve
Besteck (n)	cutlery
bestellen	to order
bezahlen	to pay
Bio-	organic
Blumenkohl (m)	cauliflower
Bockwurst (f)	frankfurter
Bohne (f)	bean
Braten (m)	roast
Bratwurst (f)	fried sausage
Brot (n)	bread
Brötchen (n)	roll
Butterbrot (n)	sandwich
Chips (pl)	crisps
Ei (n)	egg
Eisdiele (f)	ice cream parlour
Erfrischungen (pl)	refreshments
Essig (m)	vinegar
Fleisch (n)	meat
Frikadelle (f)	meatball
Fruchtsaft (m)	fruit juice
Frühstück (n)	breakfast
Gabel (f)	fork
Gasthaus (n)	inn
gemischt	mixed
Gemüse (n)	vegetable
Geschirr (n)	crockery
Getränk (n)	drink
Gewohnheit (f)	habit
Gurke (f)	cucumber
Haferflocken (pl)	porridge
Hähnchen (n)	chicken
Hauptgericht (n)	main course
Himbeere (f)	raspberry
hungrig	hungry
Imbissstube (f)	snack bar
Kakao (m)	cocoa
Kännchen (n)	pot
Käse (m)	cheese
Keks (m)	biscuit
Kellner / Kellnerin	waiter / waitress
Kohl (m)	cabbage
Kotelett (n)	chop (e.g. pork)
Kuchen (m)	cake
lecker	tasty
Löffel (m)	spoon
Mahlzeit (f)	meal

Marmelade (f)	jam
Menü (n)	set meal
Messer (n)	knife
Milch (f)	milk
Mineralwasser (n)	mineral water
Mittagessen (n)	lunch
Nachspeise (f)	dessert
Nachtisch (m)	dessert
Nudeln (pl)	pasta
Obst (n)	fruit
Pfirsich (m)	peach
Pommes (Frites)	chips
probieren	to try
Rechnung (f)	bill
Rezept (n)	recipe
roh	raw
Saft (m)	juice
Sahne (f)	cream
Salat (m)	lettuce, salad
Salz (n)	salt
satt	full up
scharf	hot (spicy)
Schaschlik (n)	kebab
Schinken (m)	ham
Schnellimbiss (m)	snack bar
Schnitzel (n)	escalope
Schweinekotelett (n)	pork chop
Selbstbedienung	self-service
Senf (m)	mustard
Soße (f)	gravy, sauce
Speisekarte (f)	menu
Speisesaal (m)	dining room
Stehcafé (n)	café (standing)
Suppe (f)	soup
süß	sweet
Süßigkeiten (pl)	sweets
Tagesgericht (n)	dish of the day
Tasse (f)	cup
Teelöffel (m)	teaspoon
Teller (m)	plate
Thunfisch (m)	tuna
Tisch (m)	table
Tischtuch (n)	tablecloth
Torte (f)	gateau
trinken	to drink
Trinkgeld (n)	tip (money)
voll	full
Vorspeise (f)	starter
Wahl (f)	choice
Wein (m)	wine
Weintraube (f)	grape
Wurst (f)	sausage
Wurstbude (f)	sausage stand
Zucker (m)	sugar
Zwiebel (f)	onion

Now try this

Think about what you have eaten and drunk today. Check that you can say it all and write it out correctly in German.

Had a look ☐　　Nearly there ☐　　Nailed it! ☐

4 Customer service and transactions

Becher (m)	mug
Ente (f)	duck
Forelle (f)	trout
geräuchert	smoked
hausgemacht	homemade
Honig (m)	honey
Kalbfleisch (n)	veal
Knoblauch (m)	garlic
Kräutertee (m)	herbal tea
Lachs (m)	salmon
Lammfleisch (n)	lamb
Meeresfrüchte (pl)	seafood
Pastete (f)	pâté
Pute (f)	turkey
Rindfleisch (n)	beef
Rührei (n)	scrambled egg
scharf	sharp, spicy
schmackhaft	tasty
Sekt (m)	sparkling wine
Spiegelei (n)	fried egg
Spinat (m)	spinach
Tablett (n)	tray
Truthahn (m)	turkey
Untertasse (f)	saucer
Vollmilch (f)	full fat milk

Zitrone (f)　　Ananas (f)　　Apfel (m)　　Birne (f)　　Erdbeere (f)

Kirsche (f)　　Pflaume (f)　　Karotte (f)　　Champignon / Pilz (m)

Erbsen (f/pl)　　Paprika (f)　　Kartoffel (f)　　Tomate (f)

Shops

Abteilung (f)	department
anprobieren	to try on
Apotheke (f)	chemist's
ausgeben	to spend (money)
Ausverkauf (m)	sale
ausverkauft	sold out
Auswahl (f)	choice, selection
Bäckerei (f)	baker's
Baumwolle (f)	cotton
billig	cheap
Blumenladen (m)	florist
Briefmarke (f)	stamp
Brieftasche (f)	wallet
Buchhandlung (f)	bookshop
Drogerie (f)	chemist's

Einkäufe (pl)	purchases
einkaufen	to shop
Einkaufskorb (m)	shopping basket
es passt dir	it fits / suits you
es steht dir	it suits you
Fischgeschäft (n)	fishmonger's
Fleischerei (f)	butcher's
Fotoapparat (m)	camera
Friseur (m)	hairdresser
Geld (n)	money
Geldschein (m)	bank note
Geldstück (n)	coin
Geschenk (n)	present
gestreift	striped
Größe (f)	size
günstig	low priced
Halskette (f)	necklace
Handtasche (f)	handbag
Hausschuh (m)	slipper
kariert	checked
Kasse (f)	till, check-out
Kaufhaus (n)	department store
Kaugummi (m)	chewing gum
Klamotten (pl)	clothes
Kleingeld (n)	small change
Konditorei (f)	cake shop
Lebensmittel (pl)	groceries
Leder (n)	leather
liefern	to deliver
Mantel (m)	coat

Marke (f)	make, brand
Metzgerei (f)	butcher's
Mode (f)	fashion
Ohrring (m)	earring
Pfand (n)	deposit (bottle)
Quittung (f)	receipt
Rabatt (m)	discount
reduziert	reduced
Regenschirm (m)	umbrella
Rolltreppe (f)	escalator
Schaufenster (n)	shop window
Schlange stehen	to queue
Schmuck (m)	jewellery
Schweinefleisch	pork
im Sonderangebot	on special offer
Tabak (m)	tobacco
teuer	expensive
Turnschuhe (pl)	trainers
Umkleidekabine (f)	changing room
Verkäufer/in	sales assistant
Warenhaus (n)	department store
Wechselstube (f)	bureau de change
Wolle (f)	wool
zahlen	to pay
zerbrechlich	fragile

Now try this

Use this page to list 10 types of shop in German and then list two items that you can buy in each shop.

④ Customer service and transactions

Etikett (n) — label
herabgesetzt — reduced
Kunststoff (m) — plastic
Mindesthaltbar-
keitsdatum (n) — best-before date
Möbelgeschäft (n) — furniture shop
preiswert — value for money
Seide (f) — silk
Sommer- / Winter-
schlussverkauf — summer / winter sale
Tante-Emma-Laden — corner shop
Verpackung (f) — packaging

Clothes

Anzug (m) — suit
Badeanzug (m) — swimming costume
Badehose (f) — trunks
Handschuh (m) — glove
Jacke (f) — jacket
Klamotten (fpl) — clothes
Kleidung (f) — clothing
Kostüm (n) — suit
Mütze (f) — cap
Nachthemd (n) — nightdress
Schlafanzug (m) — pyjamas
Slip (m) — pants, briefs
Stiefel (m) — boot
Strumpfhose (f) — tights
Unterhose (f) — underpants

Bademantel (m) — dressing gown
Pantoffel (m) — slipper
Schlips (m) — tie
Strickjacke (f) — cardigan

Gürtel (m)

Kleid (n)

Schal (m)

Hemd (n)

Krawatte (f) / Schlips (m)

Schuh (m)

Hut (m)

Rock (m)

Socke (f)

Bluse (f)

Kapuzenjacke (f)

Jeans (f)

Regenmantel (m)

Shorts (pl)

Trainingsschuhe (m/pl)

Dealing with problems

Bedienung (f) — service
behalten — to keep
Brieftasche (f) — wallet
Dieb (m) — thief
Diebstahl (m) — theft
Fundbüro (n) — lost property
kaputt — broken
Konto (n) — bank account
krank — ill
Krankenhaus (n) — hospital
Krankenwagen (m) — ambulance
Krankheit (f) — illness
Polizeiwache (f) — police station
Personalausweis (m) — ID card

Portemonnaie (n) — purse
schade — pity, shame
sich beschweren — to complain
verlieren — to lose
Wahrheit (f) — truth
Wechselgeld (n) — change
Wechselkurs (m) — exchange rate

beschädigen — to damage
beweisen — to prove
fertig werden mit — to deal with
Gefängnis (n) — prison
verschwinden — to disappear
Versicherung (f) — insurance

Now try this

Think of all the clothes items on this page that you have worn during the past week. Make a list in English then try to write the German equivalents without looking at the page. Check back to see how many you got right. Learn those you got wrong!

⑤ Future plans, education and work

Basic language of the internet

Bildschirm (m)
Tastatur (f)
Taste (f)
Computer (m)
Drucker (m)
Maus (f)

brennen	to burn
drucken	to print
herunterladen	to download
hochladen	to upload
Kennwort (n)	password
löschen	to erase
Schrägstrich (m)	forward slash
speichern	to save
tippen	to type
Verbindung (f)	connection
Webseite (f)	webpage

Affenklammer (f)	at (@)
Datei (f)	(data) file
Unterstrich (m)	underscore
weltweit	worldwide

Simple job adverts

Antwort (f)	reply, answer
Anzeige (f)	advert
Arbeit (f)	work
Arbeitserfahrung (f)	work experience
Arbeitsstunden (pl)	hours of work
Ausbildung (f)	training
Bewerbung (f)	application
Brief (m)	letter
Firma (f)	company
pro Stunde	per hour
sich bewerben	to apply
Stelle (f)	job
Stellenangebote (pl)	vacancies
Stellenanzeige (f)	job advert

Simple job applications and CV

Abschlusszeugnis (n)	leaving certificate
Arbeitspraktikum (n)	work experience
beilegen	to enclose
Beruf (m)	profession, job
Eindruck (m)	impression
erfahren	experienced
Erfolg (m)	success
erfolgreich	successful
Lebenslauf (m)	CV
Lehre (f)	apprenticeship
qualifiziert	qualified
schicken	to send
Schulabschluss (m)	school certificate
Schulbildung (f)	school education
Termin (m)	appointment
Universität (f)	university
Unterschrift (f)	signature
Zeugnis (n)	school report

| Bewerbungs- formular (n) | application form |
| Vorstellungs- gespräch (n) | job interview |

School and college

Abitur (n)	Abitur (A levels)
AG (f)	school club
Anspitzer (m)	sharpener
Aufgabe (f)	task, exercise
aufpassen	to pay attention
Aula (f)	school hall
Austausch (m)	exchange
Berufsberater	careers adviser
bestehen	to pass (exam)
Biologie (f)	biology
Bleistift (m)	pencil
Chemie (f)	chemistry
Chor (m)	choir
dauern	to last
Deutsch	German
Direktor (m)	headteacher
durchfallen	to fail (exam)
Englisch	English
Erdkunde (f)	geography
Etui (n)	pencil case
Fach (n)	subject

Mathematik
Englisch
Geschichte
Kunst
Chemie
Musik

Now try this

Pick 10 words from this page that you would use when applying for a job. Memorise them and then test yourself later.

⑤ Future plans, education and work

faul	lazy
Ferien (pl)	holidays
Filzstift (m)	felt tip
fleißig	hard-working
Fortschritt (m)	progress
Frage (f)	question
Französisch	French
Fremdsprachen	languages
Füller (m)	fountain pen
Gang (m)	corridor
gerecht	fair
Gesamtschule (f)	comprehensive
Geschichte (f)	history
Grundschule (f)	primary school
Gymnasium (n)	grammar school
Hauptschule (f)	secondary school
Hausaufgaben (pl)	homework
Hausmeister (m)	caretaker
Heft (n)	exercise book
Informatik (f)	ICT
Kantine (f)	canteen
Klassenarbeit (f)	class test
Klassenfahrt (f)	school trip
Klassenzimmer (n)	classroom
Klebstoff (m)	glue
klug	clever
korrigieren	to correct
Kuli (m)	ballpoint pen
Kunst (f)	art
Kurs (m)	course
Labor (n)	laboratory
Latein	Latin
Lehrer (m)	teacher
Lehrerzimmer (n)	staff room
Leistung (f)	achievement
lernen	to learn
Lineal (n)	ruler
Mannschaft (f)	team
Mathe(matik) (f)	maths
Medienwissen-schaft	media studies
Mittlere Reife (f)	GCSE equivalent
mündlich	oral
Naturwissen-schaften (pl)	sciences
Note (f)	grade
Oberstufe (f)	sixth form
Pause (f)	break
Physik (f)	physics
Privatschule (f)	private school
Prüfung (f)	exam

Radiergummi (m)	rubber
Realschule (f)	secondary school
rechnen	to calculate
Rechner (m)	calculator
Regel (f)	rule
Schere (f)	scissors
Schreibtisch (m)	desk
schriftlich	written
Schule besuchen	to attend school
Schüler (m)	pupil
Schülermitverant-wortung (f) (SMV)	student council
schulfrei	no school
Schulhof (m)	playground
Schultasche (f)	school bag
schwach	weak (subject)
schwer	hard, difficult
Seite (f)	page
Sekretariat (n)	school office
sitzen bleiben	to repeat year
Sommerferien (pl)	summer holidays
Spanisch	Spanish
Sprache (f)	language
staatlich	state
stark	strong
studieren	to study
Stunde (f)	lesson, hour
Stundenplan (m)	timetable
Tafel (f)	board
Taschen-rechner (m)	calculator
Theater (n)	drama
Trimester (n)	term
Turnen (n)	gymnastics
Turnhalle (f)	gym
üben	to practise
Übung (f)	exercise
Umkleideraum (m)	changing room
ungerecht	unfair
Unterricht (m)	lesson
unterrichten	to teach
Versammlung (f)	assembly
weitermachen	to carry on
Werken (n)	DT
wiederholen	to repeat
Wörterbuch (n)	dictionary
zeichnen	to draw
Zettel (m)	note
Zukunftspläne (pl)	future plans

H HIGHER

abschreiben	to copy
abwesend	absent
anwesend	present
Aufsatz (m)	essay
Aussprache (f)	pronunciation
begabt	gifted
Besprechung (f)	meeting
„blau" machen	to skive
Entfernung (f)	distance
Ergebnis (n)	result
erklären	to explain
hitzefrei	time off due to heat
Hochschule (f)	university
Internat (n)	boarding school
Jura	Law
Klassenbuch (n)	class register
Kopfhörer (pl)	headphones
lehren	to teach
nachsitzen	to have detention
notwendig	necessary
Pflichtfach (n)	core subject
schwänzen	to skive
Strafarbeit (f)	lines (punishment)
streng	strict
Studium (n)	studies
übersetzen	to translate
vereinbaren	to agree
Wahlfach (n)	optional subject
Wirtschaftslehre (f)	economics

1 = sehr gut	very good
2 = gut	good
3 = befriedigend	satisfactory
4 = ausreichend	adequate
5 = mangelhaft	poor, unsatisfactory
6 = ungenügend	inadequate

Now try this

What GCSEs are you and your friends taking? Check that you can say / write all the subjects in German. If you're thinking of taking A levels, can you name those subjects too?

⑤ Future plans, education and work

Work and work experience

Add –in for the female word, unless given.

Angestellter/ Angestellte	employee
Anruf (m)	call
Arbeiter (m)	worker
Arbeitgeber (m)	employer
Arbeits- bedingungen (pl)	terms of employment
arbeitslos	unemployed
babysitten	to babysit
Bäcker (m)	baker
Bauarbeiter (m)	builder
Bauer (m)	farmer
Beamter (m)	civil servant
Beamtin (f)	civil servant
Begeisterung (f)	enthusiasm
berufstätig	in work
beschäftigt	busy
Besitzer (m)	owner
Betrieb (m)	business
Bezahlung (f)	pay
Blumenhändler (m)	florist
Briefmarke (f)	stamp
Briefträger (m)	postman
Chef (m)	boss
einstellen	to appoint
Elektriker (m)	electrician
Fabrik (f)	factory
Fehler (m)	mistake
Ferienjob (m)	holiday job
feuern	to fire
Feuerwehrmann	fireman
Fleischer (m)	butcher
Ganztagsjob (m)	full-time job
Gehalt (n)	salary
Gelegenheit (f)	opportunity
geplant	planned
Hausfrau (f)	housewife
Hausmann (m)	house husband
jobben	to do casual work
Kassierer (m)	cashier
Kaufmann (m)	businessman
Kauffrau (f)	businesswoman
Klempner (m)	plumber
Kollege / Kollegin	colleague
Künstler (m)	artist

der Arzt   die Ärztin

die Krankenschwester
der Krankenpfleger

der Friseur   die Friseuse

der Polizist   die Polizistin

die Gärtnerin   der Gärtner

der Zahnarzt   die Zahnärztin

Lehrling (m)	apprentice	Reisebüro (n)	travel agency
Lkw-Fahrer (m)	lorry driver	Schauspieler (m)	actor
Lohn (m)	wage(s)	Schichtarbeit (f)	shiftwork
Maler (m)	painter	schlecht bezahlt	badly paid
Maurer (m)	builder	selbstständig	independent
Messe (f)	trade fair	Soldat (m)	soldier
Metzger (m)	butcher	Sorge (f)	worry
Mitteilung (f)	message	Stadtführer (m)	city guide
Nachricht (f)	message	Streik (m)	strike
Nebenjob (m)	part-time job	Teilzeit (f)	part time
Polizei (f)	police		

Now try this

To help you learn the jobs vocabulary, make a list of five jobs that you would like to do and five jobs that you would not like to do and then memorise them.

⑤ Future plans, education and work

Tellerwäscher (m)	washer-upper	Auszubildende (m/f)	trainee
Tierarzt (m)	male vet	Bewerber (m)	applicant
Tierärztin (f)	female vet	Dolmetscher (m)	interpreter
Tischler (m)	joiner	Einzelhändler (m)	retailer
verdienen	to earn	Fließband (n)	conveyer belt
Verkäufer (m)	sales assistant	freiwillig	voluntary
Vertreter (m)	representative	Gelegenheits-	casual work
Werkstatt (f)	workshop	arbeit (f)	
Zeitungen	to deliver	Gesetz (n)	law
austragen	newspapers	Gleichheit (f)	equality
Ziel (n)	aim	Gleitzeit (f)	flexitime
zurückrufen	to call back	kündigen	to resign
		Landwirt (m)	farmer
		Rechtsanwalt (m)	lawyer
		Schriftsteller (m)	author
		sich entschließen	to decide
Arbeitnehmer (m)	employee	Unternehmen (n)	firm
Arbeitsamt (n)	job centre	vereinbaren	to agree
ausrichten	to give a message		

HIGHER H

New vocabulary

Now try this

Use the space on this page to note down and revise any other useful words you've found during your course.

Answers

Personal information

1. Birthdays
1 **(a)** 30. Oktober 1983
2 **(b)** 17. Mai 1989
3 **(c)** 29. März 1979

2. Physical description
1 **(c)** long dark brown hair
2 **(b)** a goatee and an earring
3 **(a)** a scar

3. Character description
Thomas's characteristics: messy, lazy, generous, understanding

4. ID
First name: Alex
Surname: Schmidt
Age: 18
Date of birth: 17. März 1994
Place of birth: Berlin
Postcode: D-11179

9. General hobbies
1 **(b)** Television
2 **(a)** Music
3 **(c)** Reading

11. Arranging to go out
1 the swimming pool
2 to do homework
3 the sports centre
4 no money

12. Last weekend
Last weekend: **(b)** Shopping, **(f)** Ice-skating, **(a)** Reading
Next weekend: **(e)** Music, **(c)** Going to a party

13. TV programmes
Past: **(b)** Cartoons
Present: **(a)** Music shows **(c)** Documentaries
Future: **(d)** The news

16. Online activities
(a) Because her parents think it is very important
(b) Chat
(c) Funny pictures from school

19. Eating at home
(a) neither
(b) supper
(c) supper

20. Healthy eating
(a) Being vegetarian – present
(b) Roller skating – past
(c) Hiking – future

23. Health problems
(a) Susanne
(b) Susanne
(c) Grandad
(d) Lukas

Out and about

25. What to do in town
Nina: **(a)** Shopping, **(d)** Wander round, **(e)** Go to the cinema
Karl: **(b)** Swimming, **(c)** Meet friends

26. Signs around town
1 **(c)**
2 **(a)**
3 **(b)**
(b) Georg (klingeln – to ring)

27. At the station

	→	↔	Depart	Arrive
1		x	7:30	8:40
2	x		16:04	20:10
3		x	12:03	14:22
4	x		19:30	21:15

28. Weather
1 **(b)** will lessen on Tuesday
2 **(a)** will be colder than the coast

29. Places in town
Cinema, Church, Dancing, Rollerblading

30. Around town
1 One of the most popular tourist destinations in Germany
2 Beautiful, small
3 Historic buildings, e.g. town hall and castle gate (Burgtor)
4 In the town centre

Town description
Dortmund **(c)** West
Hamburg **(b)** North
Dresden **(a)** East
Munich **(e)** South
Kassel **(d)** Central

35. Holiday homes
1 Television
2 Broken

36. Staying in a hotel
1 **(c)** gym
2 **(b)** entertained
3 **(a)** return to the same hotel

37. Staying at a campsite
(a) Tent and caravan pitches
(c) Modern wash facilities
(e) Drinking fountains
(f) Boat hire

39. Holiday activities
day trips, climbing, walking, theme park, archery

40. Booking accommodation
(a) Ich möchte bitte vom ... bis ... ein Doppelzimmer reservieren. Ich hätte, wenn möglich, gern ein Zimmer mit Seeblick.
(c) Ich möchte bitte vom ... bis ... ein Einzelzimmer reservieren. Ich hätte, wenn möglich, gern ein Zimmer mit Vollpension / Halbpension.

42. Past holidays
1 **(c)** – negative
2 **(a)** – positive
3 **(b)** – negative
4 **(d)** – positive

43. Directions
(a) Zum Marktplatz gehen Sie hier gleich links und dann über die Kreuzung.
(c) Zum Marktplatz gehen Sie hier gleich rechts und dann um die Ecke.

45. Transport
1 Much better than in England
2 If we invested more in trains

Customer service and transactions

46. At the café
Mohammed **(e)**
Martin **(c)**
Christian **(b)**
Didi **(a)**
Markus **(d)**

47. Eating in a café
1 Oliver: A
2 Susanne: C

48. At a coffee house
1 Strong – einen starken Espresso
2 Daily – Ihre tägliche Tasse
3 Milk – mit oder ohne Milch

49. At a restaurant
1 Large selection of dishes
2 Price of set meal / starter, main and dessert

50. Food opinions
1 Rude
2 Wonderful view and 10% student discount

52. Shops
(a) Musikgeschäft – music (3)
(b) Delikatessengeschäft – deli items (1)
(c) Elektrogeschäft – electrical goods (4)
(d) Möbelgeschäft – furniture (2)

53. At the market
(a) cucumber
(c) raspberries
(f) carrots

54. Food shopping
Sophie bought a jar of honey for €4.99.

56. Shop signs
(a) 4 Lift out of order
(b) 3 Summer sale starts
(c) 5 Open daily from nine to six
(d) 1 Pay here

57. Clothes and colours
1 Olga – jacket
2 Fatima – trousers
3 Sophie – skirt
4 Lisa – gloves
5 Anja – jumper

59. Returning clothes
1 (a) is damaged
2 (b) get his money back
3 (d) at home
4 (g) work

61. Shopping opinions
(b) The top end shops were not popular.
(d) Lukas enjoys shopping in his free time.

63. Money problems
1 Mrs Gruber (b) spent too much money
2 Mr Gruber (a) lost a credit card
3 Martin (d) did not like English food
4 Julia (c) had to visit the doctor

64. Problems at the station
(a) Elena
(b) Hanna
(c) Sara
(d) Toby

65. Lost property
1 wallet
2 about a quarter past eleven
3 black
4 women's department

Future plans, education and work

67. School subjects
1 Geography
2 Learnt a lot
3 Learnt vocabulary for the English test

69. School routine
(b) Beth is reluctant to get up.
(c) School is compulsory.
(e) Beth has to do some work on the journey.
(f) Beth has to be in class at ten past eight.

71. Primary school
(c) in different ways

72. Issues at school
1 Ralf (b) 34° draußen – heute ist hitzefrei.
2 Teresa (d) Die Ergebnisse der Klassenarbeit sind hier zu finden.
3 Frau Scheer (e) Bitte nicht eintreten: Besprechung.
4 Pupils (f) Schreibt bei den Abschlussprüfungen nicht ab!
5 Dietmar (c) Elternabend der 13. Klasse: 1. Mai um 20:00 Uhr.

74. Future careers
1 Lothar (d) excitement
2 Ercan (e) money
3 Maria (c) outdoor work
4 Knut (a) travel
5 Saskia (b) teamwork

75. Jobs
1 2
2 Nurse
3 No
4 Doctor, long hours
5 Programmer / IT person, works from home

76. Job adverts
(a) Plumber – 2
(b) Computer expert – 4
(c) Sales assistant – 1
(d) Vet – 3

78. Job application
1 (a) excellent
2 (c) a tourist information office
3 (a) tiring
4 (c) go abroad

80. Opinions about jobs
1 Positive
2 Negative
3 Positive
4 Positive
5 Negative
6 Positive
7 Positive
8 Negative
9 Negative
10 Positive

83. Work experience
1 (a) Last week
2 (b) In a travel agent's
3 (b) Tired
4 (c) A police officer

84. Dialogues and messages
1 (c) the pool
2 (e) late
3 (d) white trainers
4 (b) train

85. Language of the internet
1 (c) Rat geben
2 (a) viel Geld gekostet

Grammar

87. Gender and plurals
(a) die Anmeldung / die Anmeldungen
(b) der Fahrer / die Fahrer
(c) das Rührei / die Rühreier
(d) die Haltestelle / die Haltestellen
(e) der Fernseher / die Fernseher
(f) das Brötchen / die Brötchen

88. Cases 1

(a) gegen die Mauer

(b) außer einem Kind

(c) trotz des Schnees

(d) nach einer Stunde

(e) zu den Geschäften

(f) ohne ein Wort

(g) während des Sommers

(h) beim Arzt

89. Cases 2

(a) der

(b) den

(c) dem

(d) die

(e) der

(f) den

(g) den

(h) die

90. Cases 3

(a) I don't want to go shopping.

(b) She spent all her pocket money on clothes.

(c) Such people quickly become impolite.

(d) I find my life boring.

(e) This time we are going by train.

(f) His parents are unemployed.

(g) I find such rules stupid.

(h) Which book are you reading?

91. Adjective endings

(a) ausgezeichnete

(b) warmes

(c) preisgünstiges

(d) zentrale

(e) beliebte

(f) meistverkauften

(g) verkaufsoffenen

(h) persönlichen

92. Comparisons

(a) einfacher

(b) jünger

(c) besser

(d) nützlicher

(e) winzigste

(f) langweiligste

(g) beliebteste

(h) schlechtesten

93. Personal pronouns

(a) sie

(b) mir

(c) dir

(d) uns

(e) mir, ihm

(f) mir

94. Word order

Possible answers:

(a) Ich fahre gern ins Ausland.

(b) Man findet Informationen beim Verkehrsamt.

(c) Normalerweise esse ich gesund.

(d) Manchmal sehen wir im Jugendklub Filme.

(e) Im Juli möchte ich im Sportzentrum arbeiten.

(f) Letztes Jahr habe ich in einem Büro gearbeitet.

(g) Morgen gehe ich mit meiner Mutter ins Kino.

95. Conjunctions

(a) Ich habe bei meiner Großmutter gewohnt, während meine Mutter im Krankenhaus war.

(b) Ich bin ins Café gegangen, nachdem ich ein T-Shirt gekauft habe.

(c) Ich war in Spanien im Urlaub, als ich einen neuen Freund kennengelernt habe.

(d) Er ist sehr beliebt, obwohl er nicht sehr freundlich ist.

(e) Ich werde für eine neue Gitarre sparen, wenn ich einen Nebenjob finde.

(f) Ich bin froh, dass ich gute Noten in der Schule bekommen habe.

(g) Ich muss meine Eltern fragen, ob ich ins Konzert gehen darf.

(h) Er hat mir gesagt, dass er mit mir ins Kino gehen will.

96. More on word order

1 (a) Ich fahre nach Italien, um meine Verwandten zu besuchen.

(b) Ich gehe zum Sportzentrum, um 5 Kilo abzunehmen.

2 (a) Ich versuche, anderen zu helfen.

(b) Ich habe vor, auf die Uni zu gehen.

3 (a) Das ist das Geschäft, das Sommerschlussverkauf hat.

(b) Hier ist eine Kellnerin, die sehr unhöflich ist.

97. The present tense

(a) höre

(b) schläft

(c) geht

(d) Isst

(e) fahren

(f) machen

(g) Gibt

(h) bleibt

98. More on verbs

1 (a) Ich sehe fern. Ich habe ferngesehen.

(b) Ich steige um sechs Uhr um. Ich bin um sechs Uhr umgestiegen.

(c) Ich lade Musik herunter. Ich werde Musik herunterladen.

(d) Ich habe abgewaschen. Ich muss abwaschen.

2 (a) mich

(b) uns

(c) euch

(d) sich

99. Commands

To pay attention to their darlings and not to use the green spaces and paths as a dog toilet.

100. Present tense modals

(a) Ich muss um einundzwanzig Uhr ins Bett gehen.

(b) In der Schule darf man nicht rauchen.

(c) Du sollst den Tisch decken.

(d) Kannst du mir zu Hause helfen?

(e) Ich will in den Ferien Ski fahren.

(f) Ich möchte am Wochenende fernsehen.

(g) Ich kann das Problem nicht lösen.

101. Imperfect modals

1 (a) Ich musste Hausaufgaben machen.

(b) Sie konnten mir nicht helfen.

(c) Er wollte eine neue Hose kaufen.

(d) Wir sollten das Zimmer aufräumen.

(e) In der Schule durfte man nie Kaugummi kauen.

(f) Alle Schüler mussten bis sechzehn Uhr bleiben.

2 (a) Es könnte schwierig werden.

(b) Ich möchte das Geld auf mein Konto einzahlen.

102. The perfect tense 1

(a) Ich habe eine Jacke gekauft.

(b) Wir sind nach Ungarn geflogen.

(c) Ich habe meinen Freund gesehen.

(d) Lena und Hannah sind in die Stadt gegangen.

(e) Ich habe meine Tante besucht.

(f) Ich bin im Hotel geblieben.

(g) Was hast du zu Mittag gegessen?

(h) Am Samstag hat er Musik gehört.

103. the perfect tense 2

(a) Ich habe zu viele Kekse gegessen.

(b) Haben Sie gut geschlafen?

(c) Wir haben uns am Bahnhof getroffen.

(d) Ich war krank, weil ich den ganzen Tag gestanden habe.

(e) Ich weiß, dass du umgestiegen bist.

(f) Warum hast du die E-Mail geschrieben?

(g) Ich habe ihr empfohlen, dass sie nicht mitkommen sollte.

(h) Ich war sehr traurig, als er gestorben ist.

104. The imperfect tense

(a) Sie hatte Angst.

(b) Es war hoffnungslos.

(c) Wo tat es dir weh?

(d) Hörtest du das?

(e) Plötzlich kam uns der Mann entgegen.

(f) Das war eine Überraschung, nicht?

(g) Es war niemand zu Hause.

(h) Sie spielten gern Tischtennis.

105. The future tense

(a) Ich werde das Spiel gewinnen.

(b) Wir werden in den Freizeitpark gehen.

(c) Sie werden eine große Wohnung mieten.

(d) Ihr werdet große Schwierigkeiten haben.

(e) Er wird die Prüfung bestehen.

(f) Nächste Woche werden wir umziehen.

(g) Wirst du dich heute schminken?

(h) Ich werde mich um sechs Uhr anziehen.

106. The conditional

(a) Ich würde gern ins Theater gehen.

(b) Er würde nie spät ankommen.

(c) Wir würden nie Drogen nehmen.

(d) Würden Sie mir bitte helfen?

(e) Zum Geburtstag würde sie am liebsten Geld bekommen.

(f) Nächstes Jahr würden sie vielleicht heiraten.

(g) Wenn Latein Pflicht wäre, würde ich auf eine andere Schule gehen.

(h) Wenn ich das machen würde, gäbe es Krach mit meinen Eltern.

107. The pluperfect tense

(a) Ich hatte zu Mittag gegessen.

(b) Sie hatten als Stadtführer gearbeitet.

(c) Warst du schwimmen gegangen?

(d) Wir waren in Kontakt geblieben.

(e) Sie waren mit dem Rad in die Stadt gefahren.

(f) Ich hatte sie vor einigen Monaten besucht, aber damals war sie schon krank.

(g) Bevor ich ins Haus gegangen war, hatte ich ein Gesicht am Fenster gesehen.

(h) Obwohl ich kaum mit ihm gesprochen hatte, schien er sehr freundlich zu sein.

108. Questions

1 (a) Lesen Sie gern Science-Fiction-Bücher?

(b) Finden Sie Ihre Arbeit anstrengend?

(c) Möchten Sie nur Teilzeit arbeiten?

(d) Werden Sie nächsten Sommer nach Australien auswandern?

2 (a) Wer ist/Wie heißt Ihr Lieblingssänger?

(b) Wann sind Sie zum letzten Mal ins Theater gegangen?

(c) Warum sind Sie Lehrer(in) geworden?

(d) Wie oft essen Sie im Restaurant?

(e) Was für Geschäfte mögen Sie besonders?

109. Time markers

(a) Seit drei Jahren spiele ich Klavier.

(b) Letzte Woche hat er die Hausaufgaben nicht gemacht.

(c) Nächsten Sommer werden wir in den Bergen wandern gehen.

(d) Am Anfang wollten wir das Betriebspraktikum nicht machen.

(e) In Zukunft wird man alle Lebensmitteln elektronisch kaufen.

(f) Ich hoffe, eines Tages Disneyland zu besuchen.

(g) Vorgestern hatte ich Halsschmerzen.

(h) Früher haben sie oft Tennis gespielt.

110. Numbers

(a) 14.–23. Mai

(b) 07:45

(c) €3,80

(d) 27. Januar 1756

(e) €185 Millionen

(f) 15% Ermäßigung

(g) 16:35

(h) 35 Grad

Vocabulary p. 116

(a) 2 **(b)** 7 **(c)** 8 **(d)** 5
(e) 10 **(f)** 4 **(g)** 3 **(h)** 6
(i) 9 **(j)** 1

Published by Pearson Education Limited, Edinburgh Gate, Harlow, Essex, CM20 2JE.

www.pearsonschoolsandfecolleges.co.uk

Copies of official specifications for all Edexcel qualifications may be found on the Edexcel website: www.edexcel.com

Text © Pearson Education Limited 2013
Audio recorded at Tom Dick and Debbie Productions © Pearson Education Limited
MFL Series Editor: Julie Green
Edited by Frances Reynolds and Sue Chapple
Typeset by Kamae Design, Oxford
Original illustrations © Pearson Education Limited 2013
Illustrated by KJA Artists
Cover illustration by Miriam Sturdee

The right of Harriette Lanzer to be identified as author of this work has been asserted by her in accordance with the Copyright, Designs and Patents Act 1988.

First published 2013

16 15 14 13
10 9 8 7 6 5 4 3 2

British Library Cataloguing in Publication Data
A catalogue record for this book is available from the British Library

ISBN 978 1 446 90342 1

Copyright notice
All rights reserved. No part of this publication may be reproduced in any form or by any means (including photocopying or storing it in any medium by electronic means and whether or not transiently or incidentally to some other use of this publication) without the written permission of the copyright owner, except in accordance with the provisions of the Copyright, Designs and Patents Act 1988 or under the terms of a licence issued by the Copyright Licensing Agency, Saffron House, 6–10 Kirby Street, London EC1N 8TS (www.cla.co.uk). Applications for the copyright owner's written permission should be addressed to the publisher.

Printed in Slovakia by Neografia

Acknowledgements
The publisher would like to thank the following for their kind permission to reproduce their photographs:

(Key: b-bottom; c-centre; l-left; r-right; t-top)

Alamy Images: David Crausby 44r, Photos12 14; Corbis: KIYOMI YAMAJI / amanaimages 30; Masterfile UK Ltd: 66br; Pearson Education Ltd: Sophie Bluy 38l, 61, 63, 69, 70, 72, 82t, 82r, 106l, 106r, Jules Selmes 30r, 62, 66c; Rex Features: Sipa Press 29; Shutterstock.com: Alexander Kalina 59c, Alexander Raths 75, 109, Andre Blais 97, Chrislofoto 35, Dana E. Fry 6, Dmitriy Shironosov 12, Ilja Mašík 38c, Imants O. 44c, infografick 55, Joshua Haviv 41, Maksym Gorpenyuk 34, Martin Valigursky 33, Masson 3, Mikhail Tchkheidze 60, Paul Cowan 47, shock 10, Stephen Mcsweeny 59r, Ulrich Willmünder 86, Yan Lev 36, Yauhen Buzuk 52, Yuri Arcurs 100; The Kobal Collection: Walt Disney / Vaughan, Stephen 102; Veer/Corbis: Martinan 64; www.imagesource.com: 39

All other images © Pearson Education Limited

Every effort has been made to contact copyright holders of material reproduced in this book. Any omissions will be rectified in subsequent printings if notice is given to the publishers.

In the writing of this book, no Edexcel examiners authored sections relevant to examination papers for which they have responsibility.